Favorite Swedish Recipes

Edited by
Selma Wifstrand

DOVER PUBLICATIONS, INC.
NEW YORK

This Dover edition, first published in 1975, is an
unabridged republication of the work originally
published by Esseltes Göteborgsindustrier AB under
the title *Swedish Food.* The color plates are reproduced here in black and white.

International Standard Book Number: 0-486-23156-9
Library of Congress Catalog Card Number: 74-20441

Manufactured in the United States of America
Dover Publications, Inc.
180 Varick Street
New York, N.Y. 10014

Contents

Preface

When the Editor of this book visited the United States in 1945 she found a marked interest for an illustrated Swedish Cookbook in the English language, containing typical and well known Swedish dishes.

Thus, *Swedish Food* was planned and the idea of the book won first prize in its group in a tourist souvenir contest sponsored by the Swedish Tourist Traffic Association, the Swedish Handicrafts Association and AB Nordiska Kompaniet, Stockholm, in 1946.

Swedish Food is the work of the Home Economics Department of the Publisher in cooperation with Mrs. Emmie Berg, a former resident of Montclair, N.J., who has compiled the recipes especially for this book. They are partly based on *Stora Kokboken* by Edith Ekegårdh and Britta Haggren, a leading Swedish Cookbook issued by this Publisher. All recipes have been tested and the pictures set up in the Department's own kitchens by an expert staff, and some have also been tested by a Home Economics Consultant in the United States. Miss Greta Strömbäck, on the editorial staff of the Publisher, has supervised the work.

The Publisher and the Editor wish to express their gratitude to all those who have contributed to the planning and production of this book, which we hope will find its way to many English speaking homes interested in Swedish culinary art.

SELMA WIFSTRAND
Editor

Introduction

The Publisher of this book believes that you will enjoy making or renewing your acquaintance with Swedish food. Besides the famous smörgåsbord, with all its delicacies and appetizing tid-bits, the Swedish kitchen boasts specialities of other kinds. For in a country so far north, with a relatively severe climate, food and the preparation of food are regarded as important. Culinary imagination and skill are highly developed in Sweden and both housewives and professional cooks, aware that good, well-prepared food is always appreciated, take pride in their handiwork.

This book makes it possible for you to prepare 200 of the best Swedish dishes, breads and cookies in your own kitchen. If you cannot find some typically Swedish recipe here, it may be because one or more of the ingredients is hard to obtain outside Sweden, or because preparation of the dish is so complicated that only experienced cooks would care to undertake it. Our object has been to include dishes which are within the scope of the average person. Some time you may want to eat a Swedish meal or invite your friends to a Swedish party. You will find some suggestions for Swedish menus at the end of the book.

Our first object in publishing this book has been to afford you gastronomic pleasure, but we also hope to stimulate an interest in Sweden and the Swedish people. Besides good food, Sweden offers you a beautiful, ever-changing landscape; ideal terrain for sport and recreation; highly developed industry; and an ancient, cultivated way of life integrated with an effective, vital modern society which has been able to develop for nearly 150 years in peace.

The recipes in this book are clear, detailed and copiously illustrated. Even a beginner can follow them with ease.

The name of each dish is given in English and Swedish.

Except when otherwise indicated, all recipes serve four.

The sauce or other foods which usually accompany each dish are given in addition, a menu list suggests other delicious mealtime combinations.

When capital letters are used in the text, as in "serve with Mashed Potatoes", there are recipes for the dishes mentioned in the book.

The amounts in the recipes are given in American standard measurements. For other measurements use this table of equivalents.

1 cup liquid = 1½—2 gills
1 ,, butter = ½ lb
1 ,, flour = 4½ oz.
1 ,, sugar (scant) = 7 oz.
1 cake compressed yeast = 1 oz.
1 tablespoon unflavored gelatin thickens 1 cup liquid.

All measurements are level.

Except when otherwise indicated, "flour" means "all-purpose flour".

Finally, some good advice — read each recipe all through before you start so that you know how to proceed.

CONVERSION TABLES FOR FOREIGN EQUIVALENTS

DRY INGREDIENTS

Ounces	Grams	Grams	Ounces	Pounds	Kilograms	Kilograms	Pounds
1 =	28.35	1 =	0.035	1 =	0.454	1 =	2.205
2	56.70	2	0.07	2	0.91	2	4.41
3	85.05	3	0.11	3	1.36	3	6.61
4	113.40	4	0.14	4	1.81	4	8.82
5	141.75	5	0.18	5	2.27	5	11.02
6	170.10	6	0.21	6	2.72	6	13.23
7	198.45	7	0.25	7	3.18	7	15.43
8	226.80	8	0.28	8	3.63	8	17.64
9	255.15	9	0.32	9	4.08	9	19.84
10	283.50	10	0.35	10	4.54	10	22.05
11	311.85	11	0.39	11	4.99	11	24.26
12	340.20	12	0.42	12	5.44	12	26.46
13	368.55	13	0.46	13	5.90	13	28.67
14	396.90	14	0.49	14	6.35	14	30.87
15	425.25	15	0.53	15	6.81	15	33.08
16	453.60	16	0.57				

LIQUID INGREDIENTS

Liquid Ounces	Milliliters	Milliliters	Liquid Ounces	Quarts	Liters	Liters	Quarts
1 =	29.573	1 =	0.034	1 =	0.946	1 =	1.057
2	59.15	2	0.07	2	1.89	2	2.11
3	88.72	3	0.10	3	2.84	3	3.17
4	118.30	4	0.14	4	3.79	4	4.23
5	147.87	5	0.17	5	4.73	5	5.28
6	177.44	6	0.20	6	5.68	6	6.34
7	207.02	7	0.24	7	6.62	7	7.40
8	236.59	8	0.27	8	7.57	8	8.45
9	266.16	9	0.30	9	8.52	9	9.51
10	295.73	10	0.33	10	9.47	10	10.57

Gallons (American)	Liters	Liters	Gallons (American)
1 =	3.785	1 =	0.264
2	7.57	2	0.53
3	11.36	3	0.79
4	15.14	4	1.06
5	18.93	5	1.32
6	22.71	6	1.59
7	26.50	7	1.85
8	30.28	8	2.11
9	34.07	9	2.38
10	37.86	10	2.74

The Smörgåsbord

There are three words which every visitor to Sweden learns: "skål", "tack" and "smörgåsbord". The last of these is an old tradition said to have originated long ago at country parties to which each guest brought some kind of food. All these foods were arranged on a long table around which the guests walked, filling their plates. The Smörgåsbord is still a popular institution, but today, when people have less time for preparing food, it is served only on special occasions and varies greatly in size. Sometimes it may consist only of bread, butter, herring and cheese, or it may be replaced entirely by three canapés. When eating the Smörgåsbord one always begins with bread, butter and herring, accompanied by a small glass of ice-cold brännvin. Beer is also served.

The dishes in this chapter are typical of the Swedish Smörgåsbord. Many of them may be served separately, principally as hors d'œuvre or luncheon dishes. The plates following page 24 show how the Smörgåsbord is arranged, and further suggestions for Smörgåsbords of various sizes are given on page 144.

Pickled Salt Herring

Pickled Salt Herring   *Inlagd Sill*

1 large salt herring   2 tablespoons onion, chopped
Dressing: 6 white peppercorns, crushed
$^1/_2$ cup white vinegar   6 whole allspice, crushed
2 tablespoons water   *Garnish:*
$^1/_4$ cup sugar   sliced onion or chopped chives

Clean fish, removing head, and soak overnight in cold water. Bone
and fillet. Cut in small slices, then slide spatula under slices and
arrange like whole fish on glass plate. Mix ingredients for dressing
and pour over. Garnish with sliced onion or chopped chives and
leave for 2—3 hrs. in refrigerator.

Chef's Pickled Herring   *Glasmästarsill*

2 large salt herrings   2 red onions, sliced
$^1/_4$ tablespoon whole allspice, $^1/_2$ carrot, sliced
   crushed   *Dressing:*
2 bay leaves   1 cup white vinegar
$1^1/_2$ whole ginger $^1/_3$ cup water
$^1/_2$ teaspoon mustard seed $^1/_2$ cup sugar
1 small piece horseradish, diced

Herring Salad

Clean fish, removing heads, and soak overnight in cold water. Drain dry on absorbent paper. Cut crosswise in $^1/_2$ inch slices and place together with dry ingredients in glass jar. Mix vinegar, water and sugar and bring to boiling point. Chill, pour over herring and let stand overnight in refrigerator. Always serve from jar.

Herring Salad   *Sillsallad*

1 salt herring	4 tablespoons vinegar
1$^1/_2$ cups boiled potatoes, diced	2 tablespoons water
1$^1/_2$ cups pickled beets, diced	2 tablespoons sugar
$^1/_3$ cup pickled gherkin, diced	white pepper to taste
$^1/_2$ cup apples, diced	*Garnish:*
$^1/_4$ onion, chopped	1—2 hard boiled eggs, parsley

Clean fish, removing head, and soak overnight in cold water. Drain, skin and fillet. Dice fillets, potatoes, beets, apples, onion and gherkin and mix thoroughly but carefully. Blend vinegar, sugar and pepper well and add to mixture, stirring gently. If desired, $^1/_2$ cup whipped cream may be added. Pack into mold which has been rinsed in cold water. Chill in refrigerator. Unmold and garnish with hard

Pickled Fresh Sardines or Smelts

boiled eggs cut in sections and parsley. Serve with sour cream beaten stiff, colored if desired with pickled beet juice.

Marinated Fresh Sardines or Smelts   *Marinerad strömming*

2 lbs. fresh sardines or smelts
2—3 tablespoons dill, chopped
Dressing:
¹/₂ tablespoon salt
1 tablespoon sugar
white pepper to taste

1 teaspoon French mustard
¹/₂ cup olive oil
¹/₄ cup white vinegar
2 tablespoons water
Garnish:
dill sprigs

Clean, skin and fillet fish. Rinse well under cold running water and drain. Sprinkle dill on bottom of bowl and alternate layers of fillets and dill. Mix remaining ingredients and pour over fish. Place in refrigerator 3—4 hrs. Garnish with dill sprigs and serve cold.

Pickled Fresh Sardines or Smelts   *Inkokt strömming*

2 lbs. fresh sardines or smelts
dill
Stock:
¹/₂ cup white vinegar
1 cup water
5 white peppercorns

5 whole allspice
1 bay leaf
2 teaspoons salt
2 teaspoons sugar
dill

Clean fish and rinse under cold running water. Drain, split and bone. Put a dill sprig on each fish, roll tight; place rolls close together in low saucepan. Bring stock ingredients to boil, pour over fish

and simmer 6—8 min. Watch very carefully lest fish boil to pieces. Remove gently to serving dish, strain stock and pour over. Chill and garnish with dill. If molded shape is preferred, stir ¹/₂ tablespoon gelatine into each cup strained stock. Serve cold with Smörgåsbord or as luncheon dish.

Fish in Aspic
Fisk i gelé

2—2¹/₂ lbs. salmon, mackerel or eel

To every qt. water:

1 tablespoon white vinegar
³/₄ tablespoon salt
5 peppercorns
5 allspice
1 bay leaf
plenty of dill

Garnish:
shrimps, eggs, tomatoes

Aspic:
1 pint strained fish stock
1¹/₄ tablespoons gelatine
2 egg whites
salt, white pepper

Mix all ingredients for fish stock and allow to cook 15 min. Clean and cut fish in about 1″ slices. Cook in stock about 10 min., drain and put on platter. Allow to cool.

Soak gelatine in cold water, then beat with egg whites and fish stock. Pour mixture into saucepan and bring slowly to boiling point, stirring constantly. Cover and allow to stand beside stove 15 min. Strain, adding salt and pepper to taste. Chill.

Make attractive pattern in bottom of mold with hard boiled eggs cut in sections, tomatoes and small cooked shrimps. Pour some of

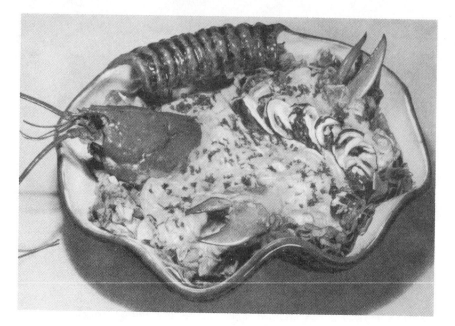

Lobster Salad

aspic over slowly and chill until liquid jellies. Arrange cold fish carefully on top and pour over remaining aspic. Chill until jellied and serve with mayonnaise on Smörgåsbord, or as luncheon dish.

Boiled Lobster *Kokt hummer*

1 lobster	*Garnish:*
3 qts. water	dill sprigs, parsley, lettuce,
¹/₂ cup salt	sliced lemon
dill	

Bring water, salt and dill to boiling point. Plunge live lobster head first into vigorously boiling water. Cover. Cook lobster weighing 2 lbs. 25 min., 1 lb. 15 min., ¹/₂ lb. 12 min. Allow to cool in stock. Split lobster and crack claws; remove dark intestinal vein and stomach. Arrange on platter and garnish with parsley, dill, lettuce and lemon slices. Serve with mayonnaise or dressing (see page 52), toast and butter.

Lobster Salad *Hummersallad*

Remove lobster meat. Cube or slice and blend with mayonnaise. Place in salad bowl and garnish with claws and lettuce leaves.

16

Preparing Herring au Gratin

Creamed Lobster

Hummerstuvning

1 boiled lobster *or* 1 can lobster meat
2 tablespoons butter or lobster butter
2 tablespoons flour
1 1/3 cups cream and lobster stock
salt, cayenne pepper

Cube lobster meat. Melt butter, add flour and stir until well blended. Add cream and stock gradually while stirring. Simmer 10 min., stirring occasionally. Remove from heat, add lobster meat and season. Reheat quickly. Serve in omelet, pastry shells or vol-au-vents.

Fresh cooked or canned shrimps, crayfish or crab meat may be substituted for lobster.

Herring au Gratin

Sillgratin

2 salt herrings
6 medium-sized raw potatoes
3 large onions, sliced
white pepper to taste
4 tablespoons butter
bread crumbs

17

Preparing Anchovies au Gratin

Clean fish, removing heads, and soak overnight in cold water. Dry on absorbent paper, skin and fillet. Cut fillets lengthwise. Peel and slice onions and potatoes thinly. Butter baking dish, then arrange potatoes, herring fillets and onions in alternate rows. Sprinkle with pepper and bread crumbs and dot with remaining butter. Bake in moderately hot oven (400 ° F.) 30 min., then reduce heat to 300 ° F. and bake another 30 min. Serve immediately from baking dish.

Anchovies au Gratin   *Ansjovisgratin*

20 anchovy fillets	2 onions, sliced
4—5 medium-sized raw	3 tablespoons butter
potatoes	1¹/₂ cups cream

Sauté sliced onions in 1 tablespoon butter. Peel potatoes and cut in lengthwise strips. Butter baking dish, then add potatoes, onions and anchovy fillets finishing with layer of potatoes. Pour in a little juice from anchovy jar and dot with remaining butter. Bake in moderately hot oven (400 ° F.), adding half cream after 10 min. and remainder after another 10 min. After 30 min., reduce heat to 300 ° F. and bake for another 30 min. Casserole is ready when potatoes are soft. Serve immediately from baking dish.

Preparing Baked Fresh Sardines

Baked Fresh Sardines or Smelts *Strömminglåda*

2 lbs. fresh sardines or smelts 3 tablespoons butter
salt 2 tablespoons bread crumbs
12 anchovy fillets

Remove heads, tails, intestines and bones. Clean well under cold running water and drain. Cut anchovy fillets in pieces. Sprinkle sardines with salt and put one piece of anchovy on each. Roll and place in well buttered and bread-crumbed baking dish. Pour a little anchovy juice over sardines, dot with remaining butter, sprinkle with bread crumbs and bake in moderately hot oven (400 ° F.) until golden brown — 10—15 min. Serve from baking dish with Smörgåsbord or as main course, with boiled or fried potatoes and green salad.

Caviar paste may be substituted for anchovies. Blend 3 tablespoons canned Swedish caviar and 2 tablespoons butter until creamy and spread on sardine fillets. Proceed as described above.

19

Eggs with Mayonnaise and Shrimps

Swedish Caviar au Gratin *Kaviarlåda*

1 small jar Swedish caviar
3 tablespoons bread crumbs
1/3 cup cream

3 eggs
1 1/2 tablespoons butter
3 tablespoons chives, minced

Bring cream to boiling point and pour over bread crumbs. Add caviar, eggs and chives, stirring constantly. Pour mixture into well buttered baking dish and dot with remaining butter. Bake in moderate oven (350° F.) 25 min. Serve immediately directly from baking dish.

Eggs with Mayonnaise and Shrimps *Ägg i majonnäs med räkor*

4 hard boiled eggs
1 1/2 cups cooked shrimps
    (1 1/4 lbs.)
1/2 cup mayonnaise

1/2 cup whipped cream
Garnish:
2 tablespoons chopped chives
    or dillsprigs

Eggs with Caviar

Halve eggs and place in middle of serving dish. Remove black vein running down back of shrimps and arrange in circle round eggs. Add cream to mayonnaise, stir until well blended, then pour over eggs. Garnish with chives or dill.

Stuffed Eggs *Fyllda ägghalvor*

4 hard boiled eggs
5 tablespoons butter
10 anchovy fillets

salt, white pepper
Garnish:
parsley, tomatoes

Cut eggs in half, crosswise or lengthwise. Remove yolks carefully and put whites aside. Pass egg yolks, butter and anchovies through sieve and stir until smooth. Season to taste. Refill whites with mixture forced through pastry tube. Sprinkle each egg with finely chopped parsley and place on lettuce leaf. Arrange on platter and garnish with sliced tomatoes.

Eggs with Caviar
Ägg med kaviargrädde

2 hard boiled eggs
²/₃ cup heavy cream
3 tablespoons Swedish caviar

1¹/₂—2 tablespoons onion, finely chopped
toast

Whip cream and stir in caviar and onions. Place in mound in middle of large platter. Arrange sliced eggs around mound and border with small pieces of fresh toast. Each person spreads his own piece of toast. Illustration, page 21.

Bird's Nest
Fågelbo

4 anchovy fillets, chopped
1 tablespoon onions, chopped
1 tablespoon capers
1 tablespoon chives, chopped

1 tablespoon pickled beets, diced
1 tablespoon cold boiled potatoes, diced
2 raw egg yolks

Arrange anchovies, onions, capers, chives, pickled beets and potatoes in mounds on round serving dish, with two raw egg yolks in center.

The person starting the dish stirs the ingredients until well blended.

Anchovy Eye
Ansjovisöga

8 anchovy fillets, chopped
1 onion, finely chopped
1 raw egg yolk

Anchovy Eye,
Raw and Fried

On round serving dish arrange outer row of finely chopped anchovies and inside row of finely chopped onions. Place egg yolk in center. The person starting the dish stirs the ingredients until well blended.

Variation: Mix ingredients, melt a little butter in hot skillet and fry quickly.

Baked Omelet   *Ugnsomelett*

4 eggs
$^1/_2$ teaspoon salt
dash of white pepper

$1^1/_3$ cups cream or milk
1 tablespoon butter

Beat eggs together with seasoning and add cream. Pour into well buttered omelet pan or baking dish. Bake in moderate oven (350 ° F.) for 15—20 min. or until golden brown. Loosen with spatula and slide onto buttered saucepan cover. Slide one half onto hot platter, cover with filling and fold over. If baking dish is used pour filling over omelet. Serve immediately.

Omelet Fillings: Creamed vegetables (page 76), asparagus or spinach, Creamed Mushrooms (page 26), Creamed Lobster or Shrimps (page 17), or Creamed Sweetbreads (page 77).

Variations: Add cubed smoked ham, chopped chives or parsley to omelet mixture. Bake in baking dish. No extra filling required.

23

The Christmas Smörgåsbord

on the opposite page consists of:

Various Kinds of Bread, Butter	Pickled Beets
Anchovies	Sausages
Chef's Pickled Herring	Salt Boiled Beef
Herring Salad	Pork Sausage
Shredded Cabbage and Apples	Brown Beans
Jellied Pork and Veal	"Pot Liquor"
Roasted Spareribs	Cheese
Liver Paté	Christmas Beer
Head Cheese	

Further details about Christmas traditions regarding food are given on page 149.

The Swedish Smörgåsbord

on the following page is composed of:

Various Kinds of Bread, Butter	Pickled Fresh Cucumber
Herring, Sardines, Anchovies	Sausages
Chef's Pickled Herring	Boiled Sliced Ham
Boiled Potatoes	Radishes
Herring au Gratin	Lobster Salad
Bird's Nest	Jellied Pork and Veal
Fish in Aspic	Pickled Beets
Swedish Caviar	Boiled Salmon
Omelet with Asparagus Filling	Green Salad
Small Meatballs	Potato Salad
Sautéed Mushrooms	Fruit Salad
Kidney Sauté	Cheese

For other Smörgåsbord suggestions, see page 144.

Swedish Sandwiches

to be served as canapés or with tea or beer at informal parties.

Creamed Rochefort and Radish
Shrimps and Mayonnaise
Liver Paté, Cucumber and Olives
Smoked Salmon, Egg and Dill

Swedish Caviar and Leeks
Ham, Apple and Cherries
Roasted Veal, Cucumber, Meat-
jelly and Tomatoes.

Creamed Mushrooms $\qquad$ *Svampstuvning*

$^1/_2$ lb. mushrooms
$^1/_2$ teaspoon salt
dash of white pepper
2 tablespoons butter

2 tablespoons flour
$1^3/_4$ cups cream
1 tablespoon Sherry or Madeira

Wash mushrooms thoroughly and cut thin slice from stem end. Slice or halve lengthwise, add butter, salt and white pepper and cook covered over low heat for $^1/_2$ hr. Then add flour and cream gradually while stirring. Simmer 10 min., stirring occasionally. Season and add wine. Serve as filling in omelet or in pastry shells.

Whole Fried Onions $\qquad$ *Helstekt lök*

8 large yellow onions
1 qt. water
salt
2 tablespoons butter

1 teaspoon brown sugar
$^1/_2$ teaspoon salt
$^1/_2$ cup stock or water

Peel onions, boil in slightly salted water for 10 min. and drain. Brown butter in skillet or Dutch oven. Add onions, sprinkle with sugar and salt and brown. Add stock or water and let simmer covered until soft. Serve as Smörgåsbord dish or with roast beef.

Sautéed Mushrooms $\qquad$ *Stekt svamp*

1 lb. mushrooms
3—4 tablespoons butter

salt, white pepper
few drops lemon juice

Wash mushrooms thoroughly and cut thin slice from stem end. Brown butter in skillet, add mushrooms and sauté over low heat until soft and golden brown. Season and add lemon juice. Serve with Smörgåsbord or with meat or fish.

Pigs' Feet $\qquad$ *Kokta grisfötter*

Pigs' feet
To every qt. water:
$^3/_4$ tablespoon salt

8—10 white peppercorns or allspice

Scrape pigs' feet and clean well. Scald in hot water, scrape again and rinse. Place in kettle, cover with water and bring to boiling point. Skim and add seasonings. Simmer 3 hrs. or until tender. Remove, place in bowl, add strained stock and let cool. Then place on cold platter with jellied stock and serve with Pickled Beets (page 30).

Breaded Pigs' Feet   *Griljerade grisfötter*

Prepare pigs' feet as in recipe above. When cooked, drain and remove bones. Brush with beaten egg and turn in bread crumbs. Fry in butter until golden brown. Serve immediately with Potato Salad, see below.

Potato Salad   *Potatissallad*

6—8 medium-sized cold boiled potatoes

Dressing:

1 $^1/_2$—2 tablespoons vinegar

5—6 tablespoons olive or salad oil

1 teaspoon salt

$^1/_4$ teaspoon white pepper

2 tablespoons onions, chopped

2 tablespoons parsley, chopped

2 tablespoons chives, chopped

$^1/_2$ cup Pickled Beets (page 30), diced

Mix vinegar, oil, salt and pepper well. Slice potatoes into salad bowl and arrange onions, parsley, beets and chives in rows on top. Pour dressing over. Keep in cool place 1—2 hrs. Turn once or twice just before serving. Serve with sausages, Pigs' Feet or cold meat.

Small Meatballs   *Små köttbullar*

$^3/_4$ lb. beef, ground

$^1/_4$ lb. fat pork, ground

$^1/_3$ cup bread crumbs

1 cup water and cream

1 tablespoon onions, finely chopped

1 tablespoon butter

2 teaspoons salt

$^1/_4$ teaspoon white pepper

($^1/_2$ teaspoon sugar)

To fry:

2—3 tablespoons butter

Sauté onions in butter until golden brown. Soak crumbs in water and cream, then add meat, pork, onion and spices and mix thoroughly until smooth. Season and shape into very small balls, using 2 tablespoons dipped in cold water. Se illustration next page. Fry in butter, shaking pan continuously to make balls round. Serve hot or cold as Smörgåsbord dish.

Liver Paté

Leverpastej

1 lb. veal liver
$^1/_4$ lb. veal
$^1/_2$ lb. fat pork
1 large onion
8 anchovy fillets
4 tablespoons flour
3 eggs

1 $^1/_3$ cups cream
1 tablespoon salt
$^1/_2$ teaspoon white pepper
3—4 truffles, chopped
For mold:
$^2/_3$ lb. fat pork cut in thin slices

Wash liver and wipe dry. Cut liver, veal and fat pork in pieces and grind together with onion and anchovies 3—4 times. Force through sieve. Beat eggs, cream and flour until well blended and add gradually to liver mixture stirring vigorously. Add seasonings and truffles and continue to beat until well blended. Line oblong mold or tin with thin slices of fat pork, fill $^3/_4$ full with mixture and tie waxed paper over top. Bake in slow oven (250 ° F.) in water bath 1 $^1/_2$ hrs. Keep in mold until cold or until next day. Unmold and serve sliced with cucumbers, sliced tomatoes and bread and butter.

Jellied Veal and Pork

Fläsk- och Kalvsylta

2 lbs. lean side pork
2 lbs. veal shank
1 $^1/_2$ qts. water
2 tablespoons salt
15 white peppercorns
10 whole allspice
2—3 bay leaves

4—6 cloves
1 onion
1 carrot
white pepper to taste
2 tablespoons weak white
vinegar
$^1/_2$ tablespoon gelatine

Jellied Veal and Pork with Pickled Beets

Rinse meat quickly in hot water and place in kettle with boiling water. Bring water to boiling point again, skim and add seasonings, onion and carrot. Simmer 1¹/₂—2 hrs. or until meat is tender. Remove meat and when cold, cut in small cubes or put through grinder. Return bones to stock and cook ¹/₂ hr. Strain stock, return to kettle, add meat and cook 10—15 min. Add white pepper, vinegar and gelatine, having first soaked latter in a little cold water. Pour into molds rinsed in cold water and harden in cold place. Unmold on serving dish, cut in slices and serve with Pickled Beets (page 30).

Head Cheese   *Pressylta*

¹/₂ hog's head (about 5 lbs.)	¹/₂ bay leaf
2 lbs. lean pork	2—3 slices onion
2—2¹/₂ lbs. veal shoulder	¹/₂ carrot
1 large piece hog's rind	*Spices:*
To every qt. water:	2 tablespoons salt
1 tablespoon salt	2 teaspoons white pepper
5 whole allspice	¹/₄ teaspoon allspice
5 white peppercorns	¹/₄ teaspoon cloves
1—2 cloves	

Clean hog's head and singe off hair and bristles. Clean teeth with stiff brush and cut off ears. Soak in cold water 6—12 hrs., changing water if necessary. Place with other meat and rind in boiling water to cover. Bring water to boiling point again, skim and add remaining ingredients. Simmer 1¹/₂—2 hrs. or until tender. Remove meat and cut rind away from head.

The Kidney is cut in slices

When cold, cut all meat in thin slices. Spread cloth or towel wrung out in hot water in deep bowl and line with rind, right side down. Arrange fat and lean meat in alternate layers, sprinkling spices on each layer, and cover with pieces of rind. Pull cloth together tightly and tie securely with string. Place head cheese in saucepan, cover with stock and cook slowly 10 min. Remove to platter, cover with board and put weight on top for 24 hrs. Then remove cloth, keeping head cheese in strongly salted water. Serve sliced with Pickled Beets, see below.

Pickled Beets   *Inlagda rödbetor*

20 small beets   *Dressing:*
1 qt. water   1 cup vinegar
2 teaspoons salt   4 tablespoons water
     4 tablespoons sugar
     1 clove

Wash beets well and cut off leaves, leaving $^1/_2$ inch of stem. Place whole in boiling water with salt and cook 20—40 min. or until tender. Drain, cool, peel and cut in thin slices. Place in glass dish. Mix vinegar, water, sugar and clove and pour over. Allow to stand 1—3

Kidney Sauté with Mushrooms

hrs. before serving. Serve with Jellied Veal and Pork (page 28), Head Cheese (page 29) and other meat dishes.

Kidney Sauté

Njursauté

1 lb. veal kidney

1/2 lb. mushrooms
1 tablespoon butter
salt, white pepper

Sauté:

1—2 tablespoons butter
1 tablespoon flour
1/2 cup beef stock
2 tablespoons Madeira or Sherry
1/2 cup cream
salt, white pepper

Clean mushrooms, cut thin slice from stem end and cook slowly in butter 10 min. Season.

Remove fat and heavy veins from kidney and cut in slices or cube. Heat butter in skillet, add kidney and brown evenly. Season and add mushrooms. Sprinkle flour over mixture and stir until well blended. Then add stock, wine and cream gradually while stirring. Cook over low heat 10—15 min. and season to taste. Serve hot.

(Mushrooms may be omitted.)

Onion Casserole

4 large onions, sliced

2 tablespoons butter

1 teaspoon sugar

$^1/_3$ lb. pork, ground

$^1/_4$ lb. veal, ground

$^1/_3$ cup bread crumbs

$^3/_4$ cup cream

$^3/_4$ cup water

1 teaspoon salt

$^1/_4$ teaspoon white pepper

stock

Melt butter in skillet and sauté onions until golden brown, sprinkling with sugar. Mix meat, bread crumbs, cream and water thoroughly until smooth. Season to taste. Cover bottom of casserole with onions, spread meat on top and cover with remainder of onions. Pour some stock over, making holes in mixture to let it run down. Bake in moderate oven (375 ° F.) 25 min. Cover if crust gets too brown. Serve very hot as Smörgåsbord dish.

Main Courses

Fish is an important item in the Swedish diet, and Swedish cooks know how to make it inviting. Herring (Baltic Herring on the east coast, a small herring which corresponds to sardines or smelts) is the commonest type, and it is prepared for the table in many different ways. Salt Herring with Sour Cream and Boiled New Potatoes, Chef's Pickled Herring, Fried Salt Herring, Broiled Fresh Sardines, and Sardine Fillets are among the classic herring dishes. Besides herring, cod, mackerel, haddock, pike, perch, trout, salmon, eel and different kinds of flat fish are popular.

Meatballs, Fried Side Pork and Brown Beans, Pork and Mashed Turnips, Beefsteak with Onions, Sailors' Beef, Filled Cabbage Rolls, and Potato Dumplings with Pork are among the meat dishes most frequently served. Veal Pot Roast, Roast Beef, Roast Lamb and Reindeer prepared on top of the stove in a "Dutch oven" are also well liked, as are chicken, goose and game. Good gravies or sauces play an important part in the Swedish cuisine, and vegetables prepared in different ways are served with meat and fish dishes. Nettle Soup, Black Soup, White Cabbage Soup and Tuesday Soup are also among the specialities of the Swedish kitchen.

Pike with Horseradish Sauce

Kokt gädda med pepparrotssås

2—2 1/2 lb. pike
1/2—1 tablespoon salt to every
    qt. water

2—3 slices onion
Garnish:
parsley and tomatoes

Clean fish, wrap in cheesecloth and plunge into sufficient boiling water to cover, adding salt and onion. Simmer 20 min. Place on hot platter, garnishing with parsley and tomatoes. Serve with boiled potatoes, grated fresh horseradish and melted butter, or with Horseradish Sauce, see below.

Horseradish Sauce

Pepparrotssås

2 tablespoons butter
2 1/2 tablespoons flour
2 cups fish stock *or* 1 cup milk
    and 1 cup fish stock

salt, white pepper
3—4 tablespoons horseradish,
    grated

Melt butter in saucepan. Stir in flour, add liquid gradually and let simmer 10 min., stirring occasionally. Season. Add grated horseradish. Do not cook sauce after adding horseradish or it will taste bitter.

Boiled Salmon

Kokt lax

2 lbs. salmon
To every qt. water:
2—3 tablespoons white vinegar
1 tablespoon salt
7 white peppercorns
5 whole allspice

1 bay leaf
1 onion
1 carrot
4—5 dill sprigs
Garnish:
lemon slices, dill or parsley

Clean fish. Combine all ingredients of stock in kettle and boil, covered, 15 min. Place fish and dill in sufficient boiling stock to cover. Bring uncovered to boiling point and skim. Simmer fish, covered 15—20 min., then remove carefully and drain. Garnish with dill sprigs or parsley and lemon slices. Serve hot with Hollandaise Sauce, see below, and boiled potatoes.

May also be served cold with Smörgåsbord, chilled in strained stock with grated fresh horseradish and sour cream or with mayonnaise and garnished with tomatoes and cucumber.

Eel, mackerel or trout may be substituted for salmon.

Hollandaise Sauce
Hollandässås

2 tablespoons wine vinegar
6 white peppercorns, crushed
5 tablespoons cold water
3 egg yolks

¾ cup butter
dash of cayenne pepper or
    paprika
2 teaspoons lemon juice

Simmer vinegar, water and peppercorns until reduced by one third and strain. Pour into double boiler. Add first egg yolks and then butter, a little at a time, stirring constantly. Cook gently until sauce is smooth and thick. Season and add lemon juice. Serve immediately or, if not served immediately, keep uncovered. If sauce shows signs of curdling, add another egg yolk and beat vigorously.

Fillet of Flounder with Sauce
Fiskfiléer med sås

2—3 flounders (2—2½ lbs.)
Stock:
3 cups water
(1 cup white wine)
2—3 slices onion
1 carrot
½ bay leaf

1 sprig parsley
2 whole allspice
6 white peppercorns
2 teaspoons salt
Garnish:
lemon slices, lettuce, tomatoes,
    shrimps or dill

Fillet fish and prepare stock. Break bones in small pieces, place in kettle and add cold water and wine. Cover, bring to boiling point, skim. Add onion, carrot and seasonings. Boil covered 10 min., then strain.

Roll fillets and place in kettle. Pour in prepared stock and simmer covered 12—15 min.

Variation: Instead of fish stock, squeeze juice of half lemon mixed with 2—3 tablespoons water over fish and dot with 1 tablespoon butter.

Place fillets on hot platter. Prepare sauce and pour over. Garnish with lemon slices, lettuce, tomatoes, shrimps or dill. Serve with boiled potatoes.

Fish Sauce
Fisksås

3 tablespoons butter
1 tablespoon flour
2—3 egg yolks
½ cup heavy cream

½ cup fish stock
salt, white pepper
(2 teaspoons lemon juice)

Rolled Fish Fillets with Lemon Sauce

Melt butter in double boiler. Stir in flour and simmer 5 min. Add egg yolks, cream and fish stock gradually, stirring constantly until sauce is smooth and thick. Season. Add lemon juice if prepared fish stock is used.

Rolled Fish Fillets with Lemon Sauce   *Fiskrulader med citronsås*

1 ¹/₂ lbs. fillets of flounder   *Garnish:*
fish stock (page 35)   shrimps, dill or parsley

Roll each fillet and fasten with toothpick. Place in low kettle. Pour hot fish stock over fish, barely covering it. Simmer covered 10—15 min.

Variation: Instead of fish stock, squeeze juice of half lemon mixed with 2—3 tablespoons water over fish and dot with 1 tablespoon butter.

Place fish on hot platter, removing toothpicks. Prepare sauce and pour over. Garnish with shrimps and dill or parsley and serve with lemon sections and boiled potatoes.

Stewed Perch

Lemon Sauce
Citronsås

1 1/2 tablespoons butter   salt, white pepper
2 1/2 tablespoons flour   juice of half lemon
1/2 cup cream or milk   1 egg yolk
1 cup fish stock   2 tablespoons cream

Melt butter, stir in flour, add cream and fish stock gradually, stirring
constantly. Simmer 10 min. Season. Add lemon juice. Beat egg
yolk and cream together and pour into sauce, stirring well.

Stewed Perch
Stuvad abborre

4 medium-sized perch   1 tablespoon chives, chopped
1 teaspoon salt   2 tablespoons flour
3 tablespoons butter.   1 cup water
2 tablespoons parsley, chopped   white pepper to taste

Scale and clean fish. Cut off fins and gills with scissors. Wash well
under running water, wipe dry and sprinkle with salt and pepper.
Butter baking dish, place fish close together and sprinkle with parsley

37

Baked Pike

and chives. Mix flour and water and spread over fish. Dot with remaining butter. Cover and simmer 15—20 min. Serve from baking dish with boiled potatoes.

Baked Pike   *Ugnstekt gädda*

2—2 ¹/₄ lb. pike   *Coating:*
1 tablespoon salt   1 egg
3—4 tablespoons butter   3 tablespoons bread crumbs
1 cup water, fish stock, milk   salt
  or cream

Scale and clean fish, removing gills but not head. Rinse and wipe dry with absorbent paper. Rub with salt and place in well buttered baking dish. Brush fish with beaten egg, then sprinkle with bread crumbs and salt. Dot with remaining butter and bake in moderate oven (350° F.) 20—30 min. Baste frequently with hot water, fish stock, milk or cream. When done, fish should flake easily from bones but still be moist. Serve direct from baking dish with boiled potatoes and vegetables, or remove to hot platter and garnish with parsley and lemon slices. Strain gravy and pour over fish or serve separately.

Cod, haddock, salmon or trout may be substituted for pike.

38

Baked Eel

Ugnstekt ål

	Coating:
1 eel (about 2 lbs.)	1 egg
1/2 tablespoon salt	3 tablespoons bread crumbs
juice of half lemon	salt, white pepper
2 tablespoons butter	

Loosen skin around neck and draw off with piece of cloth held in hand. Remove head, split open and clean thoroughly. Remove backbone, being careful not to pierce meat. Dry on absorbent paper, then rub with salt and lemon juice. Brush with beaten egg. Mix bread crumbs, salt and pepper and sprinkle over. Place in well buttered baking dish and dot with remaining butter. Bake in hot oven, basting frequently and adding hot water if needed, about 40 min. if whole, or 25 min. if cut in small pieces. Serve hot or cold with boiled potatoes, salad and mayonnaise or Sharp Sauce, see below.

Sharp Sauce

Skarpsås

1 hard boiled egg yolk	dash of white pepper
1 raw egg yolk	1—2 teaspoons sugar
1/2 teaspoon mustard	1/2—1 tablespoon wine vinegar
1/4 teaspoon salt	3/4 cup whipped cream

Press cold boiled egg yolk through sieve and mix with raw egg yolk. Add seasonings. Fold in whipped cream very carefully and serve immediately. If sauce shows signs of curdling, stir in a little heavy cream until smooth again.

Sautéed Fish

Stekta fiskfiléer

10—12 fillets of fish	To fry:
salt	3 tablespoons butter
3—4 tablespoons butter	Garnish:
juice of half lemon	lemon slices, parsley
Coating:	
1 egg	
bread crumbs	

Fillet fish, clean and wipe dry. Sprinkle with salt. Dip in egg and bread crumbs. Let coating stiffen a few minutes, then melt butter in skillet and sauté fish on each side until golden brown. Remove to

39

Sautéed Fish

hot platter. Sprinkle lemon juice in skillet and pour remaining fat over fish. Garnish with lemon slices and parsley. Serve with boiled potatoes, salad and butter mixed with chopped parsley.

Fried Fresh Sardines or Smelts   *Stekt strömming*

2¹/₄ lbs. fresh sardines or smelts   *To fry:*
¹/₂ tablespoon salt   3 tablespoons butter
bread crumbs or rye or whole
   wheat flour

Clean fish, removing heads. Rinse well under cold running water and drain. Salt and dip in bread crumbs or flour, then fry in butter until nicely brown on both sides and serve with Mashed Potatoes (page 42). Small herring may be substituted for sardines.

Pickled Fried Fresh Sardines   *Inlagd stekt strömming*

2¹/₄ lbs. fried sardines (see   7 white peppercorns
   recipe above)   6 whole allspice
1 cup white vinegar   1 red onion, sliced
¹/₄ cup water   dill
¹/₂ cup sugar

Combine all ingredients and mix well. Pour over cold fried fish. Place in refrigerator 2—4 hrs. Serve as Smörgåsbord dish.

Fried Fresh Sardines

Smelt or Fresh Sardine Fillets   *Strömmingsflundror*

2 ¹/₄ lbs. fresh sardines or smelts
¹/₂ tablespoon salt
Stuffing:
2 tablespoons butter
¹/₂ cup parsley, chopped

Coating:
1 egg
bread crumbs
To fry:
3 tablespoons butter

Remove heads, tails, intestines and bones. Clean fillets well under cold running water. Drain and wipe dry on absorbent paper, then spread out skin-side down and sprinkle with salt. Use mixed butter and parsley as sandwich filling between two fillets. Dip "sandwiches" in beaten egg, then bread crumbs. Fry in butter in skillet until golden brown and serve hot with Mashed Potatoes (page 42) and salad.

Preparing Fresh Sardine Fillets

Mashed Potatoes

Potatismos

2 lbs. potatoes	salt, white pepper
2 tablespoons butter	$^1/_2$ teaspoon sugar
1 cup boiling milk	

Wash and peel potatoes and cook in slightly salted water until soft. Drain and mash, using potato masher, or put through potato ricer. Add butter and boiling milk gradually and beat until smooth. Season. Serve immediately.

Stuffed Fish

Hel fisk i kapprock

4 mackerel (about 2 lbs.)	$^1/_2$ cup chives, chopped
2 teaspoons salt	$^1/_4$ cup onion, chopped
Stuffing:	2 tablespoons lemon juice
2 tablespoons butter	*Garnish:*
$^1/_2$ cup parsley, chopped	parsley, lemon slices

Remove bones and intestines by opening back of fish. Wash well under cold running water. Dry on absorbent paper and sprinkle with salt. Mix stuffing and fill fish. Brush center of sheets of plain waxed paper with butter and place one fish on each. Fold two long edges and

Wrapping Stuffed Fish in Wax Paper before Baking.

Salt Herring with
New Potatoes

ends of paper together two or three times. Place on griddle or
frying pan. Bake in moderately hot oven (400° F.) 10—15 min.
Remove to hot platter and garnish with parsley and lemon slices.
Serve in paper jackets with boiled potatoes and salad.

Herring or trout may be substituted for mackerel.

Broiled Fresh Sardines or Smelts *Sotare*

2 lbs. fresh sardines or smelts

¹/₂ tablespoon salt

Clean fish, rinse well, drain. Sprinkle inside and outside with salt
and leave in cool place 2—3 hrs. Make good fire and place juniper
twigs dipped in water over it. Place fish on grill and broil 2 min.
on each side. Serve immediately with boiled potatoes in jackets.

Salt Herring with New Potatoes *Spicken sill med färsk potatis*

Clean salt herrings, removing heads, skin and soak overnight in cold
water. Cut in slices ¹/₂ inch thick. Slide spatula under slices and
arrange on dish to look like whole fish. Sprinkle with chopped
chives or garnish with dill sprigs. Serve chilled with sour cream
mixed with chopped chives and new potatoes boiled with dill.

Fried Salt Herring *Stekt salt sill*

2 salt herrings   3—4 tablespoons butter
bread crumbs or rye flour   ¹/₂ cup light or heavy cream
2—3 onions, sliced

Remove heads and intestines. Skin, fillet and soak fish overnight in cold water. Drain, dry on absorbent paper. Turn in bread crumbs. Melt butter in skillet and sauté sliced onions until soft. Remove onions and fry fillets golden brown. Pour cream over and simmer 1 min. Remove fillets to hot platter and pour over gravy and onions. Serve with boiled potatoes in jackets or baked potatoes. — Onions and cream may be omitted and dish served instead with Onion Sauce (page 78).

Fish au gratin   *Fiskgratin*

1¹/₂ lbs. fillets of cod, haddock,   1¹/₂—2 cups fish stock and cream
   flounder or pike   2 egg yolks
3 tablespoons lemon juice   2—3 tablespoons cold butter
1 tablespoon butter   salt, white pepper
salt, white pepper   2 tablespoons grated cheese
Sauce: *Garnish:*
2 tablespoons butter   cooked shrimps
3 tablespoons flour

Clean fish and sprinkle with salt and pepper. Place in buttered baking dish or on silver platter, pour lemon juice over, dot with butter, cover with wax paper and bake in hot oven (425° F.) 7—10 min.

Melt butter in saucepan, add flour and stir until well blended. Add cream and fish stock gradually while stirring and simmer 10 min. Remove from heat and add egg yolks and cold butter, stirring until smooth.

Garnish fish with shrimps. Season sauce to taste and pour over. Sprinkle with grated cheese. Force Duchesse Potatoes through pastry tube on edge of fish platter. Brown under broiler or in very hot oven (500° F.) 10—15 min.

Duchesse Potatoes   *Potatismos*

1 lb. potatoes   2 egg yolks
1 tablespoon butter   salt, sugar, white pepper

Peel potatoes and boil in salted water until soft. Drain and put through potato ricer or mash thoroughly. Add butter and egg yolks and beat well. Season.

Fish Mold (Serves 8) *Fiskfärs*

1 lb. ground raw fish (pike, cod or haddock)
1 scant cup butter
3 tablespoons flour
4 eggs
1 ¹/₃ cups light cream

1 cup heavy cream, whipped
1 teaspoon salt
¹/₄ teaspoon white pepper
1 tablespoon anchovy juice
For mold:
butter, bread crumbs

Add butter and anchovy juice to finely ground fish and work until smooth. Season. Beat egg yolks, flour and light cream together and add to fish mixture gradually, beating vigorously. (If mixture shows signs of curdling place bowl over boiling water and beat until smooth again.) Fold in whipped cream and stiffly beaten egg whites. Fill buttered and bread-crumbed mold ³/₄ full. Cover with wax paper and place in deep baking pan filled with boiling water. Cook in slow to moderate oven (325 ° F.) 1—1¹/₂ hrs. or until a toothpick inserted in center comes out clean. Unmold very carefully on hot platter. Garnish with cooked shrimps and parsley. Serve with melted butter, boiled potatoes and vegetables and Hollandaise Sauce (page 35) or Mushroom Sauce, see below.

Mushroom Sauce (Serves 4) *Svampsås*

¹/₄ lb. fresh or canned mushrooms
¹/₂ teaspoon salt
dash of white pepper
2 tablespoons butter

2 tablespoons flour
2 cups cream or stock and cream
salt, white pepper
1 tablespoon Sherry

Wash mushrooms thoroughly and cut thin slice from stem end. Slice or halve lengthwise. Place in saucepan, add butter and seasoning and cook covered over low heat 30 min. Add flour and cream (and stock) gradually, stirring constantly. Simmer 10 min. until sauce thickens, stirring occasionally. Season, then add wine.

Fish Soufflé *Fisksufflé*

1 cup raw fish, ground
¹/₄ cup butter
¹/₃ cup flour
1¹/₂ cups milk
4 eggs

1¹/₄ teaspoons salt
¹/₄ teaspoon white pepper
For mold:
butter, bread crumbs

45

Melt butter and stir in flour until well blended. Add milk while stirring and cook 3—4 min. Remove from fire and add egg yolks one by one, stirring vigorously 10 min. Add fish and season. Fold in stiffly beaten egg whites, then pour mixture into well buttered and bread-crumbed mold. Bake in moderate oven (350° F.) 45 min. Serve immediately in mold with Lobster Sauce (page 50), Mushroom Sauce (page 45) or Hollandaise Sauce (page 35).

Herring Pudding   *Sillpudding*

2 salt herrings	2 onions, sliced
1¹/₂ lbs. raw potatoes	3 eggs
white pepper	2 cups milk

Remove heads and intestines. Skin, fillet and soak fish overnight in cold water. Drain and cut in even slices. Clean, peel and cut potatoes in thin slices. Alternate layers of potatoes, herring and onions in buttered and bread-crumbed baking dish, sprinkling each layer with pepper and finishing with layer of potatoes. Beat eggs and milk together and pour over pudding. Bake in oven (350° F.) 30—40 min., or until potatoes are soft. Serve in baking dish with melted or browned butter.

Salmon Pudding   *Laxpudding*

Salt salmon may be substituted for herring in above recipe. Use ¹/₂ lb. salmon and chopped parsley in place of onions.

Salt Dried Cod Pudding   *Kabeljopudding*

¹/₂ lb. raw salt dried cod	2¹/₂—3 cups milk
or 1 cup cooked fish	1 tablespoon butter
²/₃ cup rice	2 eggs
1¹/₃ cups water	(salt), white pepper

Soak fish overnight in cold water. Cook, chill, bone and cut fine. Place rice in strainer and rinse under cold running water. Boil water, add rice and simmer until water disappears. Add milk and bring to boil, then cover and simmer 45 min. or until rice is tender. Mix rice with butter, fish and eggs. Season and pour into buttered and bread-crumbed baking dish. Sprinkle with bread crumbs and butter. Bake in moderate oven (325° F.) 25—30 min. Serve with melted butter. Leftovers may be sliced and fried in butter.

Soaking of Swedish "Lutfisk" (Ling)   *Beredning av lutfisk*

To every 2^1/$_2$ lbs. dried spring ling: ^{1}/$_2$ lb. soda
^{1}/$_2$ lb. slaked lime   water

To get fish ready for Christmas Eve, begin December 9th.

Divide fish in 2 or 3 pieces and put in wooden tub. Add cold water to cover and place in cool place, changing water every day for 4 days. Then scrub fish on both sides and remove. Empty tub. Cover bottom with lime; arrange layer of fish, skin-side down, on top. Cover with lime, add another layer of fish, skin-side up, and cover with lime. Dissolve soda in a little warm water; add cold water. Pour slowly over fish until very well covered. Solution should always cover all of fish. Last of all, put light press over tub (board with big stone on top).

Soak fish 5—7 days, or until soft enough to let finger penetrate thickest part easily. Remove. Rinse tub, return fish and cover with fresh cold water. Change water every day first 3 days, later twice every week. Fish is ready to cook after 4—6 days in fresh water. Cook small piece first to test. Fish may be kept in water a long time, but becomes hard if kept too long.

Crayfish Party

For menus for crayfish parties, see page 148.

Goose Dinner

For menu for goose dinner, see page 150.

Boiled "Lutfisk"

Kokt lutfisk

3 lbs. soaked lutfisk (see recipe on page 47)
salt, water

Skin and cut up fish. Place pieces close together in cheese-cloth and sprinkle with salt. Place on fish rack. Bring very slowly to boiling point and simmer 10—15 min. If fish is very soft, plunge into boiling salted water (3 tablespoons salt to every qt. water). If fish is hard, use less salt. When ready, drain and remove to hot platter. Always serve with salt, black and white pepper and mustard, boiled potatoes, melted butter and White Sauce, see below. Lutfisk may also be served with green peas. Illustration, page 47.

White Sauce

Mjölksås

3 tablespoons butter
3 tablespoons flour

2¹/₂ cups milk, or half milk and half cream
salt, white pepper

Melt butter. Add flour and stir until well blended. Add milk gradually while stirring. Cook slowly 10 min., stirring occasionally. Season.

Lobster Sauce

Hummersås

1 boiled lobster
or 1 small can lobster meat
2 tablespoons butter or lobster butter

2 tablespoons flour
1 cup fish or lobster stock
1 cup cream
salt, white pepper

Melt butter, add flour and stir until well blended. Add cream and fish stock gradually, stirring constantly. Simmer 10 min., stirring occasionally. Add lobster meat cut in pieces and season. Reheat.

Lobster Soufflé

Hummersufflé

2 lobsters
2 tablespoons butter or lobster butter
3 tablespoons flour
1¹/₃ cups cream and fish stock

4 eggs
salt, white pepper
For mold:
bread crumbs, butter

Boil lobster and split. (See directions for Boiled Lobster, page 16.) Remove and cube meat. Melt butter, add flour and stir until well

blended. Add cream and fish stock gradually while stirring. Simmer
3—4 min., then remove from fire and add egg yolks, beating vigorously 10 min. Add lobster meat and season. Fold in stiffly beaten egg
whites and pour into buttered and bread-crumbed mold or individual
casseroles. Bake in moderate oven (350° F.) 45 min. or in individual
casseroles 15—20 min. Serve in mold with melted butter or Hollandaise Sauce (see page 35).

Lobster au Gratin   *Gratinerad hummer*

2 lobsters
3 tablespoons butter or lobster
   butter
2^1/$_2$ tablespoons flour
1^1/$_3$ cups cream and fish stock
salt, dash of cayenne pepper

2 egg yolks
3 tablespoons grated Parmesan
   or Swiss cheese
Garnish:
parsley

Boil lobster and split, following directions for Boiled Lobster on
page 16. Remove and cube meat. Reserve and clean shells. Melt
butter, add flour and stir until well blended. Add cream and fish
stock gradually while stirring, then simmer 10 min., stirring occasionally. Add egg yolks and 1 tablespoon grated cheese and remove
from heat. Add lobster meat, stirring carefully. Refill shells with
mixture; sprinkle with grated cheese. Place under broiler or in moderately hot oven (400° F.) 10—12 min., or until golden brown.
Garnish with parsley and serve immediately.

Crayfish   *Kräftor*

30 crayfish
3 qts. water

6 tablespoons salt
heads of dill

It is very important that every crayfish be alive before boiling. Wash
thoroughly in cold water. Boil water, salt and dill 2—3 min., then
plunge 10—12 crayfish in at a time, bringing water back to boiling
point each time before plunging in more. Add more dill, cover
and cook 9—10 min. Cool in "pot liquor" 10—12 hrs. before
serving. Arrange on platter. Garnish with heads of dill.

The beginning of the Swedish crayfish season in August is celebrated
with special parties (see page 148). Crayfish are regarded as a great
delicacy.

Marinated Salmon ready to be covered with a weighted board.

Marinated Salmon (Serves 8)
Gravad lax

3—4 lbs. salmon
dill
²/₃ cup salt
¹/₂ cup sugar
20 white peppercorns,
  crushed
(pinch of saltpeter)

Dressing:
3 tablespoons olive or salad oil
1¹/₂ teaspoons vinegar
¹/₂ teaspoon French mustard
¹/₄ teaspoon salt
dash of white pepper
Stir dressing until well blended.

Select middle cut of 6—7 lbs. salmon. Clean and remove bone; divide in two and wipe thoroughly with cloth. Place dill in bottom of pan. Mix salt, sugar and pepper and rub into fish. To retain red color of salmon, add pinch of saltpeter to spices. Place one piece, skin-side down, in pan and sprinkle with spices and dill sprigs. Put other piece on top, skin-side up. Cover with weighted board; keep in refrigerator 16—24 hrs. Remove spices and cut in thick slices. Arrange on platter, garnishing with dill. Serve with dressing, poached eggs, buttered spinach and boiled potatoes.

Smoked Salmon
Rökt lax

Arrange slices of smoked salmon on platter. Garnish with lettuce leaves and dill sprigs. Serve with poached eggs, buttered spinach and new potatoes.

Veal Pot Roast with Vegetables

Veal Pot Roast (Serves 8) *Kalvstek*

5 lbs. leg of veal
2 tablespoons butter
1 tablespoon salt
$^1/_2$ teaspoon white pepper
2 cups weak stock or water
4 carrots, sliced
2 onions, sliced

Gravy:
5 tablespoons flour
2 cups drippings and stock
1 cup cream
salt, white pepper

Trim meat and wipe with cloth. Rub with salt and pepper. Heat butter in Dutch oven, then brown meat on all sides. Add carrots, onions and hot stock and cook slowly, covered, 1—1$^1/_2$ hrs. or until tender. Baste occasionally and add more hot stock if needed. When ready, place on hot platter and keep warm.

Strain drippings. Remove fat and heat, add flour and stir until browned. Add pan drippings, stock and cream gradually. Simmer 10 min., stirring occasionally. Season and serve separately. Garnish meat with carrots and onions and serve with Browned Potatoes, peas, Pickled Fresh Cucumber or pickled gherkin and Lingonberries.

Browned Potatoes   *Brynt potatis*

   2 lbs. boiled potatoes $^1/_2$ teaspoon salt
   2 tablespoons butter $^1/_2$ teaspoon sugar
   $^1/_2$ cup bread crumbs

Peel potatoes and shape into small balls. Brown half of butter in skillet with half of bread crumbs. Add half of potatoes, season and shake continuously until potatoes are covered with bread crumbs and nicely brown. Remove from pan and proceed in same way with remainder.

Pickled Fresh Cucumber   *Inlagd gurka*

   1 cucumber, about 7 inches   2 tablespoons sugar
     long $^1/_4$ teaspoon salt
   $^1/_2$ cup vinegar   dash of white pepper
   2 tablespoons water   1 tablespoon parsley, chopped

Wipe and slice cucumber without peeling and place in glass dish. Mix vinegar, water, sugar, salt and white pepper thoroughly, pour over cucumber and sprinkle with parsley. Allow to stand 2—3 hrs. in refrigerator before serving. Serve with meat.

Royal Pot Roast (Serves 8)   *Slottsstek*

   4 lbs. round or rump of beef   6 white peppercorns
   $^1/_2$ lb. fat pork, sliced and cut   2 tablespoons vinegar
     in strips (lardoons)   (2 tablespoons Brandy)
   2 tablespoons butter   2 tablespoons molasses
   1 tablespoon salt   *Gravy:*
   $^1/_2$ teaspoon white pepper   5 tablespoons flour
   2 cups stock or water   2 cups stock and pan drippings
   2 onions   1 cup cream
   4 anchovies   salt, white pepper
   2 bay leaves   1 tablespoon anchovy juice
   12 whole allspice

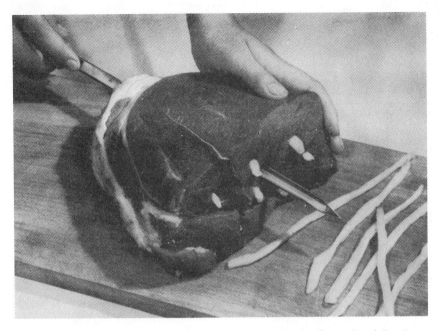

Larding a Royal Pot Roast

Trim meat and wipe with cloth. Roll lardoons in salt and white pepper. Insert lardoons in parallel rows. Rub meat with salt and pepper. Brown butter in Dutch oven, add meat and brown on all sides. Remove from heat and add hot stock or water. Then add remaining ingredients and cook slowly on top of stove about 3 hrs. or until tender. When done, place on hot platter and keep warm.

Strain pan drippings. Remove fat and heat. Add flour, stirring until browned, then add stock, pan drippings and cream gradually. Simmer 10 min., stirring occasionally. Add salt, pepper and anchovy juice. Serve separately.

Serve with vegetables and Browned Potatoes, page 54.

Swedish Pot Roast (Serves 8)   *Grytstek*

4 lbs. round or rump of beef   1 tablespoon salt
$^1/_2$ lb. fat pork, sliced and cut $^1/_4$ teaspoon white pepper
   in strips (lardoons)   (2 carrots, 2 onions)
2 tablespoons butter   2 cups stock or water

Gravy:	salt
5 tablespoons flour	white pepper
3 cups pan drippings and stock	1 tablespoon anchovy juice
or 2 cups drippings and 1 cup	
heavy cream	

Trim meat and wipe with cloth. Roll lardoons in salt and white pepper. Insert one end of lardoon into larding needle and with pointed end draw needle through, leaving lardoon in meat. Arrange lardoons in parallel rows. Rub meat with salt and pepper. Heat butter in Dutch oven and brown meat (together with carrot and onion) on all sides. Remove from heat and add hot water. Cook slowly, covered, on top of stove about 3 hrs. or until tender. Baste occasionally, adding more hot water if needed. When done, place on hot platter and keep warm.

Strain drippings. Remove fat and heat. Add flour, stirring until browned. Then add drippings and beef stock or cream gradually while stirring. Simmer 10 min., stirring occasionally. Add salt, pepper and anchovy juice. Serve separately.

Serve with vegetables and Browned Potatoes, page 54.

Swedish Pot Roast with Vegetables

Roast Leg of
Lamb with
Tomatoes and
Mushrooms

Roast Leg of Lamb (Serves 8)   *Lammstek*

4—4¹/₂ lb. leg of lamb   *Gravy:*
1 tablespoon salt   5 tablespoons flour
¹/₄ teaspoon white pepper   3 cups pan drippings and stock
1 cup water or stock   salt, white pepper
1 cup coffee with sugar and   *Garnish:*
  cream   parsley, cucumber
2 carrots
2 onions

Trim meat and wipe with cloth, then rub with salt and pepper. Place in roasting pan and roast in hot oven until nicely brown on all sides. Add carrots and onions. Reduce heat, add stock and roast in moderate oven (375 ° F.) about 2 hrs., basting occasionally. Add coffee when half done.

Strain pan drippings. Remove fat and heat. Add flour, stirring until browned. Then add drippings and stock. Simmer 10 min., stirring occasionally. Season. Serve separately.

Place lamb on hot platter. Garnish with parsley and cucumber. Serve with Browned Potatoes (page 54), Whole Fried Onions (page 26), Sautéed Mushrooms (page 26) or other vegetables if desired.

Loin of Pork with Prunes

Loin of Pork with Prunes (Serves 8)   *Plommonspäckad fläskkarré*

3¹/₂ lbs. loin of pork	¹/₂ teaspoon white pepper
20 prunes, pitted	(¹/₄ teaspoon ginger)
2—3 teaspoons salt	2 cups stock or water

Trim meat and wipe with cloth. Rinse prunes in warm water and halve. Insert prunes deeply in meat. Rub meat with seasonings and tie with string. Brown on all sides in Dutch oven. Add hot stock or water, cover and simmer over low heat about 1¹/₂ hrs. or until tender. Baste occasionally and add more hot stock if needed. When ready, place meat on hot platter, remove string, cut loose from back bone, then slice. Strain and skim pan drippings. Serve separately.

Serve with Browned Potatoes (page 54), cooked prunes, apple sauce and any desired vegetables.

If thick gravy is preferred, remove 3 tablespoons fat and heat, then add 3—4 tablespoons flour, stirring until browned. Add 2 cups pan drippings, stock and cream gradually. Simmer 10 min., stirring occasionally, and season with salt and white pepper.

Roasted Spareribs (Serves 8)   *Ugnstekt revbensspjäll*

5 lbs. spareribs, bones cracked	($^1/_4$ teaspoon ginger or pow-
1$^1/_2$ tablespoons salt	dered mustard)
$^1/_2$ teaspoon white pepper	2 cups beef stock or water

Trim meat and wipe, then rub with mixed seasonings. Brown in Dutch oven on both sides. Reduce heat, add hot beef stock or water and roast in moderate oven about 1$^1/_2$ hrs. or until meat is tender. Baste occasionally. Cut in pieces and place on hot platter. Remove fat from liquid. Strain liquid, season and serve separately. Serve with apple sauce, cooked prunes, Browned Potatoes (page 54) and vegetables or cold as Smörgåsbord dish.

Variation: Prepare spareribs as in recipe above. Rinse and halve 20 prunes and peel, core and slice 4—6 apples. Rub meat with mixed seasonings. Spread fruit over inside of ribs, roll and tie securely. Brown and roast as above about 2 hrs. When ready, carve and place on hot platter garnished with cooked prunes and apples. Remove fat from liquid. Strain liquid, season and serve separately.

Braised Whole Veal Liver   *Helstekt kalvlever*

2 lbs. veal liver	*Gravy:*
2 teaspoons salt	2$^1/_2$ tablespoons flour
$^1/_4$ teaspoon white pepper	1$^1/_2$ cups pan drippings and
1$^1/_2$ tablespoons butter	beef stock
1$^1/_2$ cups beef stock,	$^1/_2$ cup cream
or bouillon cubes and water,	salt, pepper
or water and milk	

Trim, wash and wipe liver. Rub with salt and pepper. Sear in butter in Dutch oven until evenly brown, turning with two wooden spoons. Add stock and cook slowly, covered, 50—60 min., basting occasionally. Remove, cut in thin slices, place on hot platter and keep warm.

Strain drippings. Remove fat and heat. Add flour, stirring until browned, then drippings, stock and cream. Simmer 10 min., stirring occasionally. Season to taste and pour over liver. Serve with boiled potatoes, Lingonberries and Pickled Fresh Cucumber (page 54).

Fried Whole Chicken with Green Salad

Fried Chicken

2 spring chickens
2—3 teaspoons salt
¹/₄ teaspoon white pepper
Stuffing:
3—4 tablespoons parsley,
    chopped
2 tablespoons butter

To fry:
2 tablespoons butter
³/₄ cup stock or water
Gravy:
drippings
1 tablespoon flour
1—1¹/₂ cups cream
salt, white pepper

Wipe chickens with cloth. Rub inside and out with salt and pepper. Stuff with mixed parsley and butter. Truss. Heat butter in Dutch oven and brown. Add hot stock and cook slowly, covered, 30 min. or until tender, basting occasionally.

Strain drippings. Remove fat and heat, adding flour while stirring. Then add cream and drippings gradually and simmer 10 min., stirring occasionally. Season.

Halve chickens and place on hot platter, garnishing with tomatoes and parsley. Serve with Browned Potatoes (page 54) and Mixed Green Salad, see below.

Mixed Green Salad

	Dressing:
2 heads lettuce	3 tablespoons olive oil
1 bunch radishes	1 tablespoon vinegar
2 hard boiled eggs	$^1/_2$ teaspoon French mustard
4 small tomatoes	$^1/_4$ teaspoon salt
2 tablespoons chives, chopped	dash of white pepper

Wash and dry lettuce. Break leaves into pieces and put in salad bowl. Skin tomatoes and slice; clean radishes and slice thinly. Separate egg yolks from whites and chop each coarsely. Arrange sliced tomatoes, chopped egg yolks, sliced radishes and chopped egg whites in rings on top of lettuce, with chopped chives in center.

Mix ingredients for dressing until well blended and pour over salad. Just before serving, toss lightly with salad fork and spoon until well saturated with dressing. Serve with meat or fish or as Smörgåsbord dish.

Roast Goose (Serves 8—10)   *Stekt gås*

1 young goose (10—12 lbs.)	2—2$^1/_2$ cups water or stock
1$^1/_2$ tablespoons salt	*Gravy:*
$^1/_2$ teaspoon white pepper	pan drippings
6—8 apples, peeled and cut in quarters	1—2 tablespoons cornstarch or potato flour
20 prunes, pitted	

Singe, clean, wash and dry goose. Head, neck, wingtips and giblets may be used for Black Soup (page 62). Rub inside and out with salt and pepper. Stuff with apples and prunes, sew and truss. Place breast up in roasting pan and roast in moderately hot oven (425 ° F.) 2—2$^1/_2$ hrs. Baste frequently. When almost done, baste with 2—3 tablespoons cold water to make skin brittle and leave oven door slightly open.

Strain drippings and remove fat. Mix a little water and flour and stir into drippings. Bring to boil and season to taste. Serve separately.

When goose is ready, remove string, carve, leaving slices in place, and arrange on hot platter. Garnish with fruit stuffing and parsley. Serve with Browned Potatoes (page 54), Brussels sprouts, Red Cabbage (page 62) and apple sauce.

Boiled Red Cabbage (Serves 8—10)   *Kokt rödkål*

2 large heads red cabbage, shredded or cubed

2—4 tablespoons butter

1—3 tablespoons molasses

2—3 apples, peeled and sliced

1 onion, grated

juice of one lemon

$^1/_2$ cup red wine or vinegar

salt

Melt butter in Dutch oven. Add shredded cabbage and molasses and brown over slow fire, stirring constantly. Add apples, onion, lemon juice, wine and salt. Simmer covered 1—2$^1/_2$ hrs., stirring occasionally. Season to taste. Serve with Roast Goose (page 61) or Christmas Ham (page 63).

Black Soup (Serves 10)   *Svartsoppa*

giblets of 1 goose (heart, gizzard, neck, head, wing-tips)

$^1/_2$—1 qt. water

$^1/_2$—1 tablespoon salt

1 slice onion

4—6 white peppercorns

2—4 cloves

2 cups goose or pigs' blood

3$^1/_2$ qts. beef stock and stock from giblets

3 tablespoons butter

7—9 tablespoons flour

1 tablespoon salt

6—7 tablespoons sugar

$^1/_3$—1 teaspoon white pepper

$^1/_3$—1 teaspoon ginger

$^1/_3$—1 teaspoon cloves, ground

4—6 tablespoons weak or wine vinegar

$^1/_3$ cup Brandy *or* 1 cup Burgundy, Sherry or Madeira

Garnish:

5—6 apples

24 prunes

2 cups water

2—3 tablespoons sugar

Clean and prepare giblets; soak in cold water 2—3 hrs. Reserve liver and neck skin for liver sausage. Put remainder in cold water and heat slowly to boiling point. Add seasonings and simmer 2—3 hrs. until giblets are tender. Strain, remove bone and cube. Cool stock and remove fat. Rinse and soak prunes and cook separately with peeled apples cut in sections.

Melt butter, add flour and stir until well blended. Add stock while stirring and simmer 10 min. Strain and return to kettle. Add strained blood, beating vigorously, and bring soup to boiling point, beating continuously. Remove from heat, season with spices, wine and fruit juice. Soup should be highly seasoned. Place cubed giblets, fruits and slices of Goose Liver Sausage on hot soup plates, or serve soup and arrange giblets, fruits and sliced Goose Liver Sausage on separate serving dish.

Goose Liver Sausage (Serves 10) *Gåsleverkorv*

1 goose liver	1 tablespoon onion, minced
¹/₂ lb. calf's liver	2—3 tablespoons seedless
3 tablespoons rice	raisins
¹/₂ cup water	salt, white pepper, molasses
1 cup milk	pinch of marjoram
¹/₂ tablespoon flour	neck skin of goose and sausage
2 eggs	casing

Cook rice in water and milk and cool. Pass liver through sieve and mix with remaining ingredients. Season. Sew up one end of neck skin. Fill ²/₃ of skin with mixture and sew up other end. Put remaining mixture into sausage casing. Place in low pan, cover with water and simmer uncovered 1—1¹/₄ hrs. Cut in thick slices and serve with Black Soup, see recipe above.

Christmas Ham *Kokt griljerad skinka*

10—12 lbs. ham	10 white peppercorns and
1 cup salt	allspice
¹/₄ cup sugar	*Coating:*
¹/₂ tablespoon saltpeter	1 egg white
Brine:	1 tablespoon mustard or
To every qt. water:	mustard powder
¹/₂ cup salt	2—3 teaspoons sugar
1 tablespoon sugar	bread crumbs
¹/₄ tablespoon saltpeter	*Garnish:*
To cook:	parsley, cooked prunes, apple
water	or orange sections
1—2 bay leaves	

Wipe ham, rub with mixture of salt, sugar and saltpeter, and place in clean wooden or stone crock. Allow to stand in cool place 1—3

Christmas Ham

days, turning occasionally. Make brine of boiling water, salt, sugar and saltpeter. Cool and pour over ham to cover. Weigh down with plate and leave 10 days.

Remove ham, wipe well and place fat-side up in boiling water to cover. Bring water to boiling point again and skim. Add bay leaves and pepper and cover. Simmer 3 hrs. or until tender. When cooked, skin and wipe with cloth, removing all loose fat. Cool in liquid, then brush with beaten egg white mixed with mustard and sugar and sprinkle with bread crumbs. Bake in moderate oven or under broiler until nicely brown. Strain liquid, season and use for "Dip in the Pot", see page 149.

Cover knuckle with red and white paper frill and garnish with creamed butter forced through fine pastry tube. Place on large platter and garnish with parsley, cooked prunes and cooked apple sections.

Serve cold with Smörgåsbord or sliced with Vegetables au Gratin (page 66), Vegetable Soufflé (page 65) or mixed vegetable salad, see illustration page 65.

Vegetable Soufflé

Grönsakssufflé

1 medium-sized head cauliflower
(asparagus, broccoli,
mushrooms or any vegetable
may be substituted for cauliflower)

2 tablespoons butter

3 tablespoons flour

1¹/₄ cups milk or cream and
small amount vegetable stock

3 eggs

salt, white pepper

Prepare vegetables and cook in slightly salted water until tender.
Drain. Separate cauliflower into flowerets. Melt butter in saucepan and stir in flour. Add cream and stock gradually while stirring
and cook slowly 10 min., stirring occasionally. Remove from heat.
Separate eggs. Then add yolks to sauce and beat vigorously 5—10
min. Season to taste and add vegetables. Beat egg whites until stiff
and fold carefully into mixture. Pour into well buttered and bread-
crumbed baking dish. Bake in moderate oven (350° F.) 30—40 min.
Serve from baking dish with melted butter, as separate dish or with
bacon or sausage.

Sliced Ham with Buttered Spinach

Preparing Vegetables au Gratin

Vegetables au Gratin

Grönsaksgratin

1 small head cooked cauliflower
2 cups cooked carrots, sliced
2 cups cooked peas
4 tomatoes, sliced
Sauce:
2 tablespoons butter

3 tablespoons flour
1 cup cream
1 cup vegetable stock or milk
salt, white pepper
2 egg yolks
1—3 tablespoons cheese, grated

Melt butter in saucepan and stir in flour until well blended. Add cream and stock or milk gradually while stirring and cook slowly 10 min., stirring occasionally. Remove from heat, add beaten egg yolks and season to taste.

Arrange all vegetables except tomatoes in well buttered baking dish or on silver platter. Pour sauce over and arrange slices of tomatoes in circle around edge of platter. Sprinkle salt and pepper on tomatoes and grated cheese over whole. Place under broiler or in very hot oven (500° F.) 10—15 min. or until nicely browned. Serve immediately, either as separate dish or with ham or sausage.

Boiled Lamb with Dill Sauce *Kokt lamm med dillsås*

2—2¹/₂ lbs. breast or shoulder
   of lamb
To every qt. water:
1 tablespoon salt

3—4 white peppercorns
1 bay leaf
dill sprigs

Rinse meat quickly with hot water, then place in kettle and cover with boiling water. Bring to boil, skim; add bay leaf, dill, salt and pepper. Cover and simmer 1—1¹/₂ hrs. or until tender. Cut in pieces, place on hot platter and garnish with dill. Serve with Dill Sauce, see below, and boiled potatoes.

Veal may be substituted for lamb.

Dill Sauce *Dillsås*

2 tablespoons butter
2 tablespoons flour
2 cups stock
2 tablespoons dill, chopped

1¹/₂ tablespoons vinegar
¹/₂—1 tablespoon sugar
1 egg yolk
salt

Melt butter, add flour and stir until well blended. Add stock gradually while stirring, then cook slowly 10 min., stirring occasionally. Add dill, vinegar and sugar. Season to taste. Remove from heat and add beaten egg yolk. Serve separately.

Boiled Lamb with Dill Sauce

Consommé with Dumplings *Buljong med klimp*

1 lb. chuck or shoulder	parsley sprigs
1 lb. beef shank	1 clove
2 qts. water	12 whole allspice
1¹/₂ tablespoons salt	*To clear:*
4 carrots, 2 parsnips, 2 leeks, 1 piece celery root, 2 onions	2 egg whites to every qt. stock

Rinse meat in cold running water and cube. Crack bones, place in large kettle, add meat and cold water. Cover and heat slowly to boiling point. Skim, add vegetables and spices and again bring to boiling point. Remove scum, cover and let simmer 3 hrs. Strain through double thickness of cheesecloth and store in cool place. To clear, remove fat from stock, place slightly beaten egg whites in kettle and add stock. Bring slowly to boiling point, stirring constantly, and boil 2 min. Allow to stand covered 20 min. over very low heat. Strain through several thicknesses of cheesecloth. Heat and serve with Dumplings. Use meat for Swedish Hash (page 85).

Dumplings *Klimp*

1¹/₂ tablespoons butter	1 teaspoon sugar
5 tablespoons flour	3 almonds, 1 bitter,
1¹/₂—2 cups milk	*or* 5 cardamom seeds, pounded
2 egg yolks	

Melt butter, add flour and stir until well blended. Add milk gradually while stirring. Simmer 10 min., stirring occasionally. Remove from heat, add slightly beaten egg yolks and reheat, stirring constantly. Add sugar and almonds or cardamom. Pour into bowl rinsed in cold water. Cool 1—2 hrs. Garnish with shredded almonds or chopped parsley.

Boiled Beef with Horseradish Sauce *Pepparrotskött med sås*

2—2¹/₂ lbs. chuck or brisket beef	1 parsnip
To every qt. water:	1 small piece celery root
1 tablespoon salt	1 onion
1 carrot	5 whole allspice

Rinse meat quickly in hot water and place in kettle. Barely cover with boiling water; bring again to boiling point. Skim. Add vegetables; bring again to boiling point. Skim, then add salt and allspice and simmer about 2 hrs. or until tender. Slice and place on hot platter. Garnish with vegetables and shredded horseradish. Serve with boiled potatoes and Horseradish Sauce, see below.

Horseradish Sauce   *Pepparrotssås*

1 1/2 tablespoons butter
2 tablespoons flour
1 cup meat stock
1 cup milk

2—3 tablespoons horseradish, grated
salt, white pepper

Melt butter, add flour and stir until well blended. Add stock and milk gradually while stirring and cook slowly 10 min., stirring occasionally. Season. Add grated horseradish. Do not cook sauce after adding horseradish or it will taste bitter.

Beef Tongue with Mushroom Sauce   *Oxtunga med svampsås*

1 fresh beef tongue (2 1/2 lbs.)
To every qt. water:
1 tablespoon salt
2 black peppercorns
6 white peppercorns

1 clove
1 bay leaf
1 carrot
1 small onion

Wash tongue and rinse in cold water. Place in boiling salted water, bring to boiling point and skim. Add remainder of ingredients and simmer 2 1/2 hrs. or until tender. Remove skin. Cut in thin slices and arrange on hot platter. Garnish with tomatoes and parsley and serve with boiled or Mashed Potatotes (page 42), peas and Mushroom Sauce (page 45).

Cured Goose (Serves 8—10)   *Sprängd gås*

1 young goose (10—12 lbs.)
2/3 cup salt
1/2 cup sugar

Brine:
To every qt. water:
1/3 cup salt
1/3 cup sugar

69

To cook:	$^1/_2$ bay leaf
To every qt. water:	$^1/_2$ carrot
2 black peppercorns	1 small onion
2 white peppercorns	parsley

Singe, clean, wash and dry goose. Rub inside and out with salt and sugar and keep in cold place 24 hrs. Mix brine, bring to boiling point, cool and pour over goose to cover. Keep in cold place 2—3 days, turning occasionally. Remove, drain and truss. Place breast up in boiling water. Bring again to boiling point and skim. Add remaining ingredients and simmer 2—2$^1/_2$ hrs. or until tender. Remove string, carve, leaving slices in place, and arrange on hot platter. Garnish with parsley and serve with boiled potatoes, Brussels sprouts, Red Cabbage (page 62) and Tomato Sauce, see below.

Cured Goose may also be served cold with Potato Salad (page 27) or vegetable salad with mayonnaise.

Tomato Sauce (Serves 8—10)   *Tomatsås*

3$^1/_2$ cups stock	1 tablespoon potato flour or
4—6 tablespoons tomato paste	cornstarch
salt, white pepper	$^2/_3$ cup Madeira

Simmer wine until reduced by one half. Add tomato paste and stock and bring to boil. Mix flour with a little cold stock and stir in. Bring to boiling point while stirring. Season.

Lamb Stew   *Fårstuvning*

2—2$^1/_2$ lbs. lean lamb breast	1 tablespoon salt
or shoulder	$^1/_4$ teaspoon white pepper
1—1$^1/_2$ lbs. potatoes	$^3/_4$—1 qt. water
4 carrots, sliced	parsley, chopped
2 leeks, sliced	

Wipe meat with cloth, then cut in large cubes. Peel and cut potatoes in thick slices. Place meat and vegetables in alternate layers in casserole or iron pot, sprinkling each layer with salt and pepper. Add water to cover. Simmer covered 1—1$^1/_2$ hrs. or until meat is tender. Sprinkle with parsley and serve directly from casserole.

70

Variation: Omit carrots and leeks and add instead 2 or 3 onions, 1 bay leaf and parsley sprigs.

Beef Stew   *Kalops*

2 lbs. beef chuck	3 red or yellow onions, sliced
2 teaspoons salt	10—15 whole allspice
$^1/_4$ teaspoon white pepper	2 bay leaves
2 tablespoons flour	2 cups water
$1^1/_2$ tablespoons butter	

Wipe meat with cloth, cut into thick slices or large cubes and remove sinews. Pound with meat hammer and turn in flour mixed with salt and pepper. Brown butter in Dutch oven. Add meat and onions and brown on all sides, then add bay leaves and whole allspice. Bring water to boiling point and pour over meat. Simmer covered for about $1^1/_2$ hrs. or until meat is tender. Add more water if needed. When ready, place meat in hot deep dish, strain liquid and pour over. Serve with boiled potatoes and Pickled Beets (page 30) or Lingonberries.

Sailors' Beef   *Sjömansbiff*

1 lb. beef chuck or round	white pepper
$1^1/_2$ lbs. potatoes	2—3 onions, sliced
2 tablespoons butter	1—2 cups water
1 tablespoon salt	

Wipe meat with cloth, cut in $^1/_2$-inch thick slices and pound. Peel potatoes and cut in thick slices. Sauté onions, then brown meat in butter in frying pan. Place alternate layers of potatoes, meat and onions, each layer sprinkled with salt and pepper, in casserole, finishing with potatoes. Pour a little boiling water into frying pan, stir and add liquid to casserole. Barely cover with water and simmer covered 1—$1^1/_2$ hrs. or until meat is tender. Sprinkle with chopped parsley and serve directly from casserole.

Lamb and Cabbage   *Får i kål*

$2^1/_4$ lbs. shoulder or breast of lamb	10 white peppercorns
	1 bay leaf
1 small head cabbage	2 cups water
2—3 teaspoons salt	parsley, chopped

Rinse meat in hot water and cut in large cubes. Trim cabbage and cut in large pieces. Place meat and cabbage in alternate layers in Dutch oven or iron pot, sprinkling each layer with salt and pepper. Add bay leaf and water, cover and bring to boiling point. Skim. Simmer 1$^{1}/_{2}$ hrs. or until meat and cabbage are tender. Arrange in deep serving dish and sprinkle with parsley. Serve with boiled potatoes.

Variation: If preferred, brown meat in butter and cube cabbage and brown in 1 tablespoon molasses.

White Cabbage Soup (Serves 8)   *Vitkålssoppa*

1 small head white cabbage	2 qts. pork or other stock
2 tablespoons fat or butter	6 whole allspice
$^{3}/_{4}$ tablespoon molasses or brown sugar	6 white peppercorns
	salt

Trim cabbage and cube, discarding core and tough portions, and brown in fat in kettle. Add molasses or brown sugar when cabbage is lightly browned and continue to brown a few minutes, stirring constantly. Bring stock to boiling point and add to cabbage. Season. Simmer new cabbage 30 min. Serve with small sausages, sliced, or Veal Meatballs, see below.

Veal Meatballs (Serves 8)   *Frikadeller*

$^{1}/_{2}$ lb. veal, ground	1$^{1}/_{2}$ teaspoons salt
$^{1}/_{2}$ lb. pork, ground	white pepper
4 tablespoons bread crumbs	*To cook:*
1 tablespoon onion, grated	1 qt. water
$^{1}/_{2}$ cup cream	$^{1}/_{2}$ tablespoon salt
$^{1}/_{2}$ cup water	

Mix meat and bread crumbs. Season, then add onion, cream and water gradually while stirring. Shape into small balls and test consistency by boiling a few balls slowly in salted water 3—5 min. If hard, add a little more water to mixture. Boil remaining balls and serve in White Cabbage Soup.

Swedish Beefsteak with Onions and Fried Potatoes

Swedish Beefsteak with Onions *Biff med lök*

1¹/₂ lbs. beef rump or top round (4 slices)	4—6 red onions, sliced, or 2—4 yellow onions, sliced
3 tablespoons butter	salt, white pepper

Wipe meat with cloth, cut in slices ¹/₂ inch thick and pound with meat hammer. Melt part of butter in frying pan and sauté onions until tender and nicely brown. Remove and keep warm. Season meat and fry 3—4 min. on each side in remaining butter in hot frying pan. Place on hot platter, pour gravy over and garnish with onions. Serve immediately with Fried Potatoes, see below, sprinkled with chopped parsley.

Fried Potatoes *Stekt potatis*

1¹/₂ lbs. boiled potatoes	salt, sugar
2 tablespoons butter	1 tablespoon parsley, chopped

Peel boiled potatoes and slice or cube. Brown butter in skillet, add potatoes, sprinkle with salt and sugar and fry until nicely brown. Sprinkle with parsley and serve with fried meat dishes.

73

Braised Veal Rolls

2 lbs. veal cutlets
1¹/₂ teaspoons salt
¹/₄ teaspoon white pepper
Stuffing:
2 tablespoons butter
2—3 tablespoons parsley, chopped
To braise:
2 tablespoons butter

1 onion
1 carrot
1¹/₂—2 cups weak stock or water
Gravy:
pan drippings
1 tablespoon flour
¹/₂ cup cream
salt, white pepper

Wipe meat with cloth, cut in slices and flatten with meat hammer. Mix butter and parsley. Sprinkle meat on both sides with salt and pepper and spread each slice with stuffing. Roll up and secure with toothpicks or string. Brown in butter with onion and carrot in Dutch oven or iron pan. Add some hot stock or water. Simmer covered 1 hr., or until tender. Baste occasionally, adding more hot water if needed. Remove toothpicks or string, place in hot deep serving dish and keep warm.

Strain pan drippings. Remove and heat fat. Add flour, stirring until browned. Then add pan drippings and cream gradually. Simmer 10 min., stirring occasionally. Season and pour over rolls. Serve with boiled potatoes, vegetables, Pickled Fresh Cucumber (page 54) and Lingonberries.

Variation: 1¹/₄ lbs. bacon cut into strips may be used instead of stuffing. Reduce salt.

Braised Beef Rolls

2 lbs. round steak
¹/₄ lb. fat pork or bacon, sliced and cut in strips
salt, white pepper

2 tablespoons butter
1—2 cups weak stock or water
1 tablespoon flour
¹/₄ cup cream

Wipe meat with cloth, cut in thin slices and pound lightly. Sprinkle with salt and pepper. Place one strip fat on each slice of beef and roll up, tying with string or fastening with toothpick. Sauté in butter in Dutch oven or skillet until brown. Sprinkle with flour, add hot stock or water and season. Simmer covered 1—1¹/₂ hrs. or until tender, turning occasionally. Remove strings or toothpicks and place rolls in hot deep serving dish. Mix cream and flour and add

Preparing Beef Rolls

to pan drippings, simmer 10 min. and pour over rolls. Serve with boiled or Fried Potatoes (page 73), Pickled Beets (page 30) or Lingonberries.

Meatballs
Köttbullar

¹/₂ lb. beef, ground	1 tablespoon butter
¹/₄ lb. veal, ground	2 teaspoons salt
¹/₄ lb. pork, ground	¹/₄ teaspoon white pepper
or ¹/₂ lb. beef, ground	*To fry:*
¹/₂ lb. pork, ground	2—3 tablespoons butter
1¹/₂ cup bread crumbs	*Gravy:*
1¹/₂ cups half cream and half water	pan drippings
	1 tablespoon flour
1 egg	³/₄—1 cup cream or milk
3 tablespoons onion, chopped	salt, white pepper

Meatballs with Creamed Vegetables

Melt butter in skillet and sauté onions until golden brown. Soak bread crumbs in cream and water liquid. Add meat, egg, onion, salt and pepper and mix thoroughly until smooth. Shape into balls, using 2 tablespoons dipped in cold water. Fry in butter until evenly brown, shaking pan continuously to make balls round, see illustration page 28. Remove each batch to saucepan and clear skillet with a little water, before starting next, saving gravy so obtained. When all meatballs are fried, mix flour and cream, add to gravy, stirring constantly, and let simmer 10 min. Add more milk or cream if too thick and season. Place meatballs in hot deep serving dish and pour gravy over. Serve with boiled potatoes, Browned Potatoes (page 54) or macaroni, Creamed Vegetables, see below, pickled gherkin and Lingonberries.

Creamed Vegetables
Stuvade grönsaker

3 cups vegetables, sliced (carrots, potatoes or any kind of vegetables)

2 tablespoons butter

2 tablespoons flour

$1^1/2$—2 cups vegetable stock and milk

salt, white pepper

1 tablespoon parsley, chopped

Prepare vegetables and cook in slightly salted water until tender. Drain; reserve cooking water. Melt butter in saucepan and stir in flour. Add reserved cooking water and milk gradually while stirring. Simmer 10 min., stirring occasionally. Then add vegetables and reheat. Pour into hot deep serving dish and sprinkle with parsley.

Beef à la Lindström

Biff à la Lindström

1 $^1/_4$ lbs. beef chuck or round, ground

2 egg yolks

$^1/_2$ cup cream

2 boiled potatoes, mashed

2 pickled beets, diced

1—1 $^1/_2$ tablespoons onion, chopped

2 tablespoons capers, chopped

salt, white pepper or paprika

2—3 tablespoons butter

Mix ground meat and potatoes with egg yolks and cream gradually, stirring. Then add beets, onion and capers carefully. Season; shape in cakes. Brown quickly in butter on both sides in skillet. Place on hot platter and garnish with parsley. Serve immediately with Fried Potatoes (page 73).

Creamed Sweetbreads

Stuvad kalvbräss

$^1/_2$ lb. sweetbreads

1 qt. water

$^1/_2$ tablespoon salt

2 tablespoons butter

2 tablespoons flour

1 $^1/_2$ cups sweetbread stock and cream

salt, white pepper

(few drops lemon juice, Sherry, or onion juice)

Soak sweetbreads in cold water 1 hr. Place in fresh cold salted water and bring to boil. Rinse in cold water and remove skin and tissue. Place in fresh, salted boiling water. Skim, then cook 10 min. Cube when cold.

Melt butter in saucepan, add flour and stir until well blended. Add stock and cream gradually while stirring. Cook slowly 10 min., stirring occasionally. Season. Then add sweetbreads and heat thoroughly. Serve in pastry shells, on toast or as omelet filling.

Fried Sweetbreads

Stekt kalvbräss

Prepare as in recipe above. When cold, slice and dip in beaten egg and bread crumbs. Fry in butter until golden brown on both sides. Serve with green peas. Illustration, page 78.

Fried Sweetbreads

Fried Side Pork

Stekt fläsk

1¹/₂ lbs. lightly salted or fresh
side pork
(salt, white pepper)

Cut pork in thin slices and remove rind or gash each rind edge 2 or
3 times. Place in hot skillet and fry until nicely brown on both sides.
If fresh pork is used, season.

Serve with Onion Sauce, see below, and potatoes in jackets or with
Brown Beans, Swedish Style (page 83).

Onion Sauce

Löksås

2 onions, chopped
1—2 tablespoons butter
2 tablespoons flour

2 cups milk
salt, white pepper, sugar

Simmer onions gently in hot butter in skillet until tender. Sprinkle
with flour and add milk gradually while stirring. Cook slowly 10 min.,
stirring occasionally. Season.

78

Preparing
Filled Cabbage
Rolls

Filled Cabbage Rolls

Kåldolmar

1 medium-sized head cabbage

Filling:

¹/₄ cup rice
1 cup water
1 cup milk

¹/₃ lb. beef, ground
¹/₄ lb. pork, ground
1 egg
¹/₃ cup milk or cream
2 teaspoons salt
¹/₄ teaspoon white pepper

To fry:

2 tablespoons butter
1 tablespoon brown sugar or
  molasses
2 cups stock or water

Gravy:

pan drippings
1¹/₂ tablespoons flour
¹/₂ cup cream
salt, white pepper

Discard wilted leaves and cut out core of cabbage head. Place cabbage in boiling salted water (2 teaspoons to every qt.) and cook until leaves are easily separated. Drain.

Rinse and scald rice. Bring water to boiling point, add rice and simmer until water disappears. Then add milk and cook slowly until rice is tender (30 min.), stirring occasionally. Cool and mix with ground meat, egg, milk and seasoning. Trim thick center vein of cabbage leaves and put 2 tablespoons of mixture on each leaf, fold leaf and fasten with string or toothpick. Heat butter in skillet and brown rolls on all sides. Place in Dutch oven and sprinkle with brown sugar. Rinse skillet out with a little boiling water and pour

79

over rolls. Add more stock or water, cover and cook slowly 1—1¹/₄ hrs. or until tender, basting occasionally.

Arrange in deep serving dish, removing toothpicks. Mix flour and cream and add to drippings while stirring. Simmer 10 min., adding more milk or cream if too thick. Season and pour over rolls. Serve with boiled potatoes.

Stuffed Onions   *Fylld lök*

    8—10 medium-sized yellow
      onions
    filling as in recipe above

Peel onions and boil in slightly salted water. Remove centers and fill. Place some onion leaves over hole and tie with string. Fry in skillet as in recipe above.

Pea Soup with Pork   *Ärter med fläsk*

    1¹/₂ cups dried yellow Swedish   1 lb. slightly salted side pork
      peas   (1 leek or 1 onion or marjoram
    2—2¹/₄ qts. water   or ginger)

Clean peas and soak overnight. Cook in same water, covered, bringing quickly to boiling point. Remove shells floating on top and add pork and desired seasoning. Cover and let simmer slowly until pork and peas are tender (1—1¹/₂ hrs). Remove pork, cut in slices and serve separately with mustard.

Thursday dinner: Pea Soup with Pork followed by Pancakes with Jam

Potato Dumplings with Pork

Kroppkakor

2 lbs. potatoes
1 egg yolk
$^1/_2$ cup flour
1 teaspoon salt

Filling:
$^1/_4$ lb. salt side pork
$^1/_4$ lb. smoked ham
4 tablespoons onion, chopped
To every qt. water:
1 teaspoon salt

Wash, peel and boil potatoes in slightly salted water until almost done. Drain and put through potato ricer. When cold, mix with egg yolk and flour and season. Cube pork and ham, fry in skillet and remove to platter. Sauté onions in fat until golden brown and mix with meat. Put potato mixture on floured board, make long roll and cut in 10 sections. Make hole in each and fill with meat, then close and shape into dumplings. Drop into salted boiling water and cook 15 min. Serve immediately with melted butter.

Öland Potato Dumplings

Öländska kroppkakor

1 lb. raw potatoes
1 lb. cooked cold potatoes
$^3/_4$ cup flour
$^3/_4$ cup barley flour
1 teaspoon salt
Filling:
$^1/_2$ lb. salt side pork

2 tablespoons yellow onion, chopped
$^1/_2$ tablespoon butter
1 teaspoon allspice, crushed
To every qt. water:
1 teaspoon salt

Peel raw potatoes and grate. Place in sieve held over bowl, letting water drop into bowl. Allow to stand. Pour out water and keep potato flour. Peel and mash cooked potatoes and mix with raw grated potatoes, white flour, barley flour and potato flour. Add salt to taste and work until well blended.

To make filling, cube pork and mix with chopped onions and crushed allspice.

Shape dough into hollow buns; fill lavishly with filling and press together. Buns should be round and without cracks. Cook in salted water $^1/_2$—$^3/_4$ hr. Serve immediately on hot platter with light cream or melted butter.

Pork and Brown
Beans

Brown Beans, Swedish Style
Bruna bönor

1¹/₂ cups brown beans   molasses

1—1¹/₂ qts. water   white vinegar

2 teaspoons salt

Wash beans and soak overnight. Cook slowly in same water until tender (1¹/₂—2 hrs.). Season to taste with salt, molasses and vinegar. Serve with Fried Side Pork (page 78) or Meatballs (page 75).

Liver Pudding (Serves 8)
Korvkaka

1¹/₃ cups rice   2 onions

2²/₃ cups water   5 tablespoons seedless raisins

5—6 cups milk   4 tablespoons molasses

1¹/₂—2 lbs. calf's or beef liver   salt, white pepper

¹/₂ lb. fat pork

Rinse and scald rice. Bring water to boiling point, add rice and simmer until water disappears. Then add milk and bring again to boiling point. Cover and simmer until rice is tender (30 min.), stirring occasionally. Grind liver, pork and onion. Rinse raisins in hot water. Mix all ingredients together and season to taste. Pour mixture into well buttered and bread-crumbed baking dish and bake in oven (350° F.) 1 hr. Serve hot with Lingonberries and melted butter. Slice left-overs, fry in butter and serve with Lingonberries.

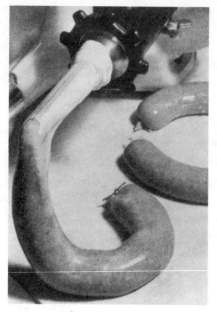

Making Pork Sausage

Pork Sausage (15 lbs.)   *Fläskkorv*

7 lbs. lean boneless pork
2 lbs. boneless veal
2 lbs. fat pork
1^{1}/4 cups potato flour
1^{1}/2—2 qts. water, or half
water and half beef or pork
stock
4^{1}/2 tablespoons salt
2 tablespoons sugar

2^{1}/2 teaspoons white pepper
2^{1}/2 teaspoons allspice
1^{1}/2 teaspoons cloves
1^{1}/2 teaspoons ginger
about 8 yds. casing
Curing:
4 tablespoons salt
4 tablespoons sugar
^{3}/4 tablespoon saltpeter

Wipe meat and run all except pork through grinder 3 or 4 times, adding fat pork last 2 times. Put ground meat in large bowl, add potato flour and knead 1 hr., adding liquid a little at a time. Then add seasonings to taste. Mixture should have consistency of firm mush.

Cut casing into 15 inches lengths and tie at ends. Fill with mixture and tie, then rinse sausages and drain on towel. Rub with curing mixture and keep in cool place. If sausage is to be kept several weeks, place in cold cooked brine (see recipe Christmas Ham page 63).

Boiled Pork Sausage

Kokt fläskkorv

2 lbs. pork sausages, recipe page 84

Place sausages in saucepan and cover with cold water. Heat slowly, reduce heat just before boiling point is reached and simmer 30 min. Remove to hot platter, cut in slices and serve with Mashed Potatoes (page 42) or Mashed Turnips (page 86) and mustard.

Swedish Hash

Pytt i panna

2 cups leftover meat, diced
2 cups boiled potatoes, diced
2 onions, chopped
3 tablespoons butter
salt, white pepper

Melt half of butter in skillet and sauté onions until golden brown. Remove to plate. Brown potatoes and then meat in remaining butter. Mix with onions and season. Arrange on hot platter and garnish with gherkin or parsley. Serve with fried eggs.

Swedish Hash with Gherkin and Fried Eggs

Mashed Turnips   *Rotmos*

1¹/₂ lbs. turnips
1 lb. potatoes
¹/₂ qt. pork stock or water

¹/₂ cup cream or stock
2 tablespoons butter
1 teaspoon sugar
salt, white pepper

Wash, peel and cube turnips and potatoes. Cook turnips in stock or slightly salted water 30 min., add potatoes and cook until soft. Drain, mash and add cream. Season. Then beat until smooth and stir in cold butter. Serve with boiled salt pork or Boiled Pork Sausage, page 85.

Potato Griddle Cakes   *Raggmunkar (Rårakor)*

1¹/₂ lbs. potatoes
1 egg
1¹/₄ cups flour
2 cups milk
1 teaspoon sugar

1 teaspoon salt
dash of white pepper
To fry:
butter or fat

Beat egg and a little of milk, then add flour and remaining milk alternately while beating. Allow to stand 2 hrs. Wash, peel and grate potatoes, then add to batter and beat thoroughly. Season. Heat griddle or frying pan, grease and cover with thin layer of batter. When browned on both sides, fold in quarters and arrange on hot platter. Serve immediately with fried salt side pork and/or Lingonberries.

Pork or Bacon Pancake   *Fläskpannkaka*

4 eggs
(salt)
1 teaspoon sugar

2 cups milk
³/₄ cup flour
¹/₂ lb. bacon or salt side pork

Sift flour into bowl; add sugar and salt. Then add eggs and milk gradually, stirring until well blended, and leave 2 hrs. Cube bacon or pork and fry in skillet or omelet pan. Beat up batter, pour over pork and bake in moderately hot oven (400° F.) 30 min. or until set and nicely brown. Cut in sections and serve with Lingonberries.

Variation: May also be fried in thin pancakes on top of stove.

Potato Griddle Cakes with Lingonberries

Vegetable Soup

Grönsakssoppa

¹/₂ head cauliflower, cut in sections	salt, white pepper
1 cup shelled peas	1 tablespoon butter
3—4 small carrots, sliced	2 tablespoons flour
5—6 cups water or beef stock	1 egg yolk
	¹/₃ cup heavy cream

Cook vegetables until tender in water or beef stock. Mix butter and flour together and add slowly to soup. Allow to simmer about 10 min. while stirring. Beat egg yolk and heavy cream together in soup tureen. Continuing to stir, pour hot soup in. Season. Sprinkle with chopped parsley and serve with cheese sandwiches.

Nettle Soup

Nässelkål

2 qts. nettles	1¹/₂ tablespoons flour
2 cups water	1¹/₄ qts. pork stock and vegetable water from nettles
salt	
1 tablespoon butter	salt, white pepper

Wash nettles well and drain. Cook in slightly salted water 10 min. or until tender. Strain, reserving water. Chop nettles finely or pass through sieve. Melt butter, add flour and stir until well blended. Add stock, still stirring, and simmer 10 min. Add nettle purée and season. Serve with poached eggs or hard boiled eggs cut in halves or sections.

Tuesday Soup

Tisdagssoppa

2 tablespoons barley	1 piece turnip
1 qt. pork stock	3—4 potatoes
2 carrots	salt, white pepper
1 parsnip	1¹/₂ cups milk
1 piece celery root	

Rinse barley in cold water and cook in stock until half done. Clean vegetables, cut in cubes and add to stock and barley. Cook until tender. Add milk, season and serve immediately.

Desserts

During the summer, Swedish housewives preserve fruits and berries for the coming winter. These preserves are used to form the basis of good everyday desserts, such as berry creams and fruit syrups. Puddings and cakes are usually served with jam. Jam is also used as a torte filling. Apple Cake with Vanilla Sauce and Sweet Pancakes with Jam are among the most popular desserts. Clabbered Milk and Shrove Tuesday Buns with Milk are also typically Swedish.

Vanilla Ice Cream (Serves 8) *Vaniljglass*

1 qt. cream
2 tablespoons vanilla extract

6 egg yolks
$^2/_3$ cup sugar

Heat cream, beat egg yolks and sugar in top of double boiler until well blended, then add cream gradually and cook until thick, stirring constantly. Add vanilla last. Pour into mold and freeze in regular freezer or refrigerator tray. Stir several times while freezing. Unmold on cold serving dish and garnish with berries, chocolate candy and whipped cream, or serve with berries and melon arranged on separate platter.

Chocolate Ice Cream *Chokladglass*

Make Vanilla Ice Cream (see recipe above) and add $1^1/_2$ oz. unsweetened chocolate to the cream before heating.

Strawberry Parfait (Serves 8) *Jordgubbsparfait*

1 cup sugar
$^1/_2$ cup water
4 egg yolks

$1^1/_2$ qts. strawberries, crushed
2 cups heavy cream, whipped

Make sugar and water syrup. Beat egg yolks in top of double boiler and pour syrup over slowly, stirring. Cook until thick, stirring constantly. Remove from heat and continue to stir until cold. Then add crushed strawberries and fold in whipped cream. Pour into freezing tray of refrigerator; allow to stand 3—5 hrs. When frozen, dip in hot water and unmold on cold platter. Garnish with strawberries and serve with fancy cookies.

Raspberries may be substituted for strawberries.

Pineapple Fromage *Ananasfromage*

1 can pineapple, cubed
juice of half lemon
$^1/_2$ cup sugar
2 eggs

$^3/_4$ tablespoon gelatine soaked
   in 2 tablespoons cold water
1 cup heavy cream, whipped

Melon and Raspberries with Vanilla Ice Cream

Pineapple Fromage

Beat egg yolks and sugar until fluffy. Add lemon, pineapple juice and gelatine dissolved over hot water to egg mixture and stir until thick. Fold in stiffly beaten egg whites, cream and pineapple cubes and pour into mold rinsed in cold water. Keep in refrigerator 3 hrs. before unmolding and serving. Garnish with pineapple slices and cherries. Serve with fancy cookies.

Lemon Fromage

Citronfromage

2 eggs
3/4 cup sugar
juice of half lemon
rind of half lemon, grated

1/2 tablespoon gelatine soaked
in 2 tablespoons cold water
1 1/4 cups heavy cream, whipped

Beat egg yolks and sugar until fluffy. Add lemon juice, rind and gelatine dissolved over hot water to egg mixture, stirring constantly until thick. Fold in stiffly beaten egg whites and cream and pour into mold rinsed in cold water. Keep in refrigerator 3 hrs. before unmolding and serving. Garnish with whipped cream and grapes. Serve with fancy cookies.

Chocolate Pudding

Chokladpudding

1 egg
1/2 cup sugar
4 tablespoons cocoa
2/3 cup cream

1/2 tablespoon gelatine soaked
in 2 tablespoons water
1 1/4 cups heavy cream, whipped

Mix egg, sugar, cocoa and cream in top of double boiler and cook until thick, beating constantly. Remove from heat, add gelatine and stir occasionally until cold. Fold in whipped cream, then pour mixture into mold rinsed in cold water. Keep in refrigerator 2—3 hrs. before unmolding and serving. Garnish with whipped cream flavored with vanilla. Serve with fancy cookies.

Caramel Pudding

Brylépudding

1 cup sugar
3 tablespoons water
3 cups cream
1 1/2 tablespoons sugar

4 eggs
1 tablespoon vanilla extract
Garnish:
blanched almonds

Melt 1 cup sugar in skillet until light brown, then add boiling water and stir constantly until syrup forms. Coat bottom and sides of ring mold or baking dish with syrup. In separate bowl, beat eggs, sugar, vanilla and cream. Pour mixture in coated baking dish. Bake in pan of hot water in slow oven (300 ° F.) 40 min. or until mixture does not adhere to knife. Cool and unmold on platter, garnish with almonds and serve with its sauce.

Chocolate Pudding

Caramel Pudding

Blucberry Pie

Blueberry Pie

Blåbärspaj

Crust:

1 cup cold, unsalted butter
1²/₃ cups flour
4 tablespoons ice-water

Filling:

1 qt. blueberries
³/₄ cup sugar

Sift flour; cut in butter with 2 knives or pastry blender. Add ice-water gradually and work dough until mixed. Chill 30 min. Roll out to rectangular shape on floured baking board, fold, repeat 2 or 3 times, then chill again. Repeat procedure twice. Wash and drain berries. Place in bowl, sprinkle with sugar and allow to stand. Divide dough in 2 portions. Roll out one portion and cover bottom of deep pie plate. Prick surface with fork to remove air bubbles and bake in hot oven (425 ° F.) 10—15 min. or until almost baked, then chill. Roll out remaining dough, line sides of plate, pressing to bottom. Fill pastryshell with blueberries. Cut remainder of rolled-out dough into strips, using pastry wheel, and arrange on top of berries, putting one strip around edge. Brush with beaten egg and bake in hot oven (425 ° F.) 20 min. until golden brown. Serve with Vanilla Sauce (page 95) or heavy cream.

Rhubarb may be substituted for blueberries.

Swedish Applecake with Vanilla Sauce

Swedish Applecake with Vanilla Sauce   *Äpplekaka med vaniljsås*

   1¹/₃ cups apple sauce   4 tablespoons butter
   2 cups zwieback crumbs or
     stale Swedish limpa, grated

Melt butter in skillet, add bread crumbs and stir until nicely brown.
Butter baking dish well and arrange crumbs and apple sauce in
alternating layers finishing with crumbs. Bake in moderate oven
(375 ° F.) 25—35 min. Cool before unmolding and serve with Vanilla
Sauce, see below.

Vanilla Sauce   *Vaniljsås*

   1 cup cream   2 teaspoons vanilla extract
   3 egg yolks   ³/₄—1 cup whipped cream
   2 tablespoons sugar

Beat egg yolks and sugar in top of double boiler. Add heated
cream and cook until thick, stirring constantly. Remove from heat,
add vanilla and cool, beating occasionally. When cold, fold in
whipped cream carefully and serve.

Apple Dumplings
Äppleknyten

10—12 sour apples	*Pastry dough:*
sugar	1 cup cold unsalted butter
cinnamon	1²/₃ cups flour
butter	4 tablespoons ice-water

Peel and core apples. Roll out pastry dough (see recipe page 94), cut in 4—5 inch squares and place apple in middle of each square. Fill apples with sugar mixed with cinnamon; dot tops with butter. Fold corners of pastry over apples, pinching edges together. Brush with beaten egg; sprinkle with sugar and chopped almonds. Bake in hot oven (425 ° F.) 5 min., then reduce heat to 350 ° F. and continue to bake until light brown. Serve hot or cold with whipped cream or Vanilla Sauce (page 95).

Filled Baked Apples
Fyllda stekta äpplen

8 apples	1—2 tablespoons water
Filling:	1¹/₂ tablespoons melted butter
¹/₂ cup blanched almonds,	sifted bread crumbs
ground	2 tablespoons sugar
¹/₄ cup sugar	

Grind almonds, then mix with sugar and water and work until smooth. Peel and core apples. Fill centers with almond paste. Roll in melted butter, then in bread crumbs mixed with sugar. Place in buttered baking dish and bake in hot oven (425 ° F.) 20—25 min. or until soft. Serve direct from baking dish with whipped cream or Vanilla Sauce (page 95).

Rhubarb Cream
Rabarberkräm

1 lb. rhubarb	2 tablespoons potato flour or
1¹/₃ cups water	cornstarch
1 cup sugar	

Clean rhubarb and cut in pieces. Bring water to boil, add rhubarb and sugar and boil until tender. Mix potato flour with small amount cold water, stir in and bring again to boil. Cool covered and serve with cream or milk.

Apple Dumplings
Ready for the Oven

Berry Cream

Berry Cream   *Bärkräm*

1 qt. berries (strawberries, raspberries, currants, gooseberries
  or blackberries)
3 cups water

3/4 cup sugar
2 tablespoons potato flour or
  cornstarch

Clean berries. Bring water to boil, add berries and sugar and boil
several minutes. Mix potato flour with small amount cold water,
stir in and bring again to boiling point. Cool covered and serve
with cream or milk.

Hip Soup
Nyponsoppa

3 cups fresh rose hips, or 2 cups dried hips

1^1/$_2$ qts. water

^{1}/$_2$ cup sugar

1^1/$_2$ tablespoons potato flour or cornstarch

Garnish:

blanched almonds

Clean rose hips and put in vigorously boiling water. Cover and cook until tender, stirring occasionally, then strain, forcing hips through sieve. Measure out 1^1/$_4$ qts. of liquid thus obtained and cold water if needed. Return to kettle, add sugar and stir in potato flour. Bring to boiling point, stirring constantly. Pour into soup tureen and add shredded almonds. Serve cold with whipped cream and Rusks (page 111).

Fruit Syrup Cream
Saftkräm

4 cups sweet fruit syrup and water, mixed

3 tablespoons potato flour or cornstarch

Bring fruit syrup and water to boil. Mix potato flour with small amount cold water, stir in and bring again to boiling point. Cool covered and serve with cream or milk.

Fruit Syrup Sauce
Saftsås

2 cups sweet fruit syrup and water, mixed

^{3}/$_4$—1 tablespoon potato flour or cornstarch

Prepare as in recipe above. Serve cold with sweet puddings.

Fruit Syrup Soup
Saftsoppa

1^1/$_2$ qts. sweet fruit syrup and water, mixed

2 tablespoons potato flour or cornstarch

Prepare as in recipe for Fruit Syrup Cream above. Serve cold with Rusks, page 111, and whipped cream.

Curd Cake   *Småländsk ostkaka*

10 qts. milk	¹/₂ cup sugar scant
²/₃ cup flour	1 pint heavy cream
3 household rennet tablets	¹/₂ cup blanched almonds,
reduced to a powder	chopped
8 eggs	

Heat milk to lukewarm. Add flour and rennet powder beating constantly. When mixture has curdled, cover and let stand 1 hr. Stir occasionally to break curd. Turn into strainer lined with cheesecloth and press out as much whey as possible. Add eggs, sugar, almonds and cream and mix well. Pour mixture into buttered mold. Bake in slow oven (250° F.) 45 min. or until firm and light brown. Serve with jam.

Swedish Pancakes   *Plättar*

1 cup flour	3 eggs
2 tablespoons sugar	3 cups milk
¹/₄ teaspoon salt	

Sift flour into bowl; add sugar and salt. Then add eggs and milk gradually, stirring until well blended, and let stand 2 hrs. Heat Swedish pancake pan (or ordinary pancake pan) and butter well. Beat batter again, pour into sections of pan and fry on both sides until nicely brown. Place on very hot platter and serve immediately with Lingonberries.

Delicatessen Waffles   *Äggvåfflor*

³/₄ cup flour	1¹/₄ cups sour cream
2 teaspoons baking powder	1 tablespoon melted butter
2 eggs, separated	

Sift flour and baking powder together, add egg yolks and cream gradually stirring until well blended. Add melted butter and fold in stiffly beaten egg whites. Brush waffle iron with butter and pour in few tablespoons of batter. Bake until golden brown, then sprinkle with sugar. Serve immediately with coffee or with jam as dessert. Illustration, page 100.

Making Waffles

Crisp Cream Waffles

Frasvåfflor

1¹/₃ cups flour   1³/₄ cups heavy cream
¹/₂ cup water   3 tablespoons melted butter

Beat cream stiff. Sift flour into cream, add cold water and stir until
well blended. Then stir in melted butter carefully. Heat waffle iron
slowly; brush generously with butter. Pour in few tablespoons of
batter and bake until golden brown. Place on rack to keep crisp.
Serve immediately with coffee or as a dessert with jam and sugar.

Poor Knights

Fattiga Riddare

12 slices stale coffee bread   ¹/₄ teaspoon salt
2¹/₂ cups milk   1 tablespoon sugar
2 eggs   ¹/₃ cup flour

Sift flour in bowl; add sugar and salt. Then add eggs and milk gradually, stirring until well blended, and let stand 2 hrs. Beat batter again.
Dip bread in milk, drain, then dip in batter. Fry in butter on both
sides until nicely brown. Serve very hot with jam.

Filled Sugar Wafers

Filled Sugar Wafers (20 wafers)   *Strutar med fyllning*

2 eggs
1¹/₄ cups powdered sugar
1¹/₄ cups flour

Filling:
1¹/₄ cups whipped cream
jam or jelly

Beat eggs and sugar until white and fluffy. Add sifted flour and stir until well blended. Drop tablespoonfuls of mixture about 3 inches apart on well greased and floured cookie sheet. Flatten out with spatula dipped in cold water to round cakes about 3 inches in diameter. Then bake in moderate oven (375 ° F.) until golden brown. Remove immediately and shape in cones, placing one inside the other in glass to keep in shape. Immediately before serving, fill with jam or jelly and top with whipped cream.

Swedish Christmas Porridge   *Risgrynsgröt*

1 cup rice
1 tablespoon butter
1 cup water

5 cups milk
1 teaspoon salt
1 tablespoon sugar

Scald rice with boiling water. Melt half of butter, add rice and water and boil 10—15 min. or until water disappears. Add milk and cook slowly 45 min. or until rice is tender. Season and add remainder of butter. Pour into deep dish and serve with cold milk, cinnamon and sugar.

Rice Pudding   *Risgrynskaka*

Add 2 eggs and ¹/₃ cup raisins to above recipe and stir until well blended. Season with grated rind of lemon, shredded almond or vanilla extract. Pour into well buttered and bread-crumbed baking dish. Bake in moderately hot oven (400 ° F.) 45 min. Serve hot or cold directly from baking dish with Fruit Syrup Sauce (page 98).

Shrove Tuesday Buns   *Semlor med mjölk*

3 cups flour
¹/₂ cup lukewarm cream
¹/₂ cup lukewarm water
¹/₂ cup butter
1 yeast cake
4 tablespoons sugar

Filling:
¹/₂ cup blanched almonds, ground
2—3 blanched bitter almonds, ground
³/₄ cup powdered sugar
1 egg white
1 cup cream, whipped

Make dough as in recipe on page 106 and allow to rise. Turn onto floured baking board and knead until smooth and firm. Shape into 12 balls. Arrange side by side on well buttered baking sheet, cover with towel and allow to rise. Brush with beaten egg and bake in hot oven (425 ° F.) until nicely brown. Cool on towel.

Mix ground almonds, sugar, egg white and a little water; work until smooth. Cut tops off buns, spread with paste and add tablespoon of whipped cream. Replace tops. Dust with powdered sugar.

Serve as dessert in deep individual dishes with hot milk, sugar and cinnamon.

Clabbered Milk   *Filbunke*

For best results in preparing clabbered milk, use fresh milk containing no preservative.

Smear bottoms of 4 individual glass or china bowls with ¹/₂ tablespoon sour cream. Set in warm place and fill with milk. Cover

Filling Shrove
Tuesday Buns

Clabbered
Milk with
Ginger Snaps

with paper and leave until milk has set. Then place in refrigerator until ready to serve. Serve with sugar, ginger and cinnamon and with Swedish knäckebröd or Ginger Snaps.

Variation: Pour all milk into large bowl. When set, chill. Beat well before serving directly from bowl.

Breads and Pastries

Delicious home-baked breads and pastries are a tradition in Sweden, and this book gives many recipes which have been handed down from generation to generation. Among these specialities are numbered Coffee Bread, Sponge Cakes, Ginger Snaps, Rye Rusks, Spritz Rings and different kinds of Puff Pastry.

At Christmas special breads and pastries are baked, including the "vörtbröd" used for "Dip in the Pot", Saffron Bread, and cookies such as Ginger Snaps, Rosettes, Christmas Crullers and Christmas Stars. Lucia Rolls, a kind of coffee bread, are served with early morning coffee on St. Lucia Day, December 13.

Coffee Bread

Coffee Bread   *Vetebröd*

8 cups flour	$^1/_2$ teaspoon salt
$2^1/_2$ cups lukewarm milk	$^3/_4$—1 cup melted butter
2 yeast cakes	(15—20 cardamom seeds,
1 cup sugar	pounded)

Dissolve yeast cakes in $^1/_2$ cup lukewarm milk. Mix remaining milk, sugar, salt, butter and cardamom seeds and small amount of flour; beat smooth. Add yeast and remaining flour, beating with wooden spoon until smooth and firm. Sprinkle dough with small amount of flour, cover with clean towel and let rise in warm place until doubled in bulk, about 2 hrs. Turn onto lightly floured baking board and knead until smooth.

To shape *Coffee Bread*

Take half of dough, divide in two or three parts and cut each part into three pieces of equal size, roll with hands into long pieces and braid. Place on buttered baking sheet, cover and let rise. Brush with slightly beaten egg. Sprinkle with sugar and chopped almonds and bake in moderate oven (375 ° F.) 15—20 min.

Preparing
Cinnamon Ring

Cinnamon Buns

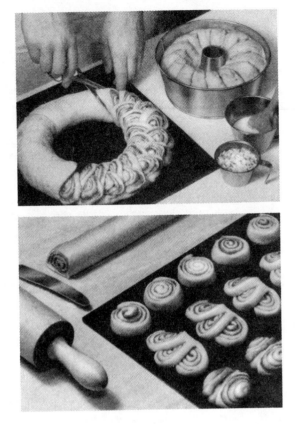

To shape *Cinnamon Ring*

Shape half of remaining dough in roll. Sprinkle baking board with flour and roll dough out as thin as possible with rolling pin. Spread with melted butter and sprinkle with sugar and cinnamon. (Ground almonds may be substituted for cinnamon.) Roll dough jelly-roll fashion, beginning at long side, and join ends to form circle. Place in buttered baking pan or sheet. Cut with scissors (see illustration) and let rise. Brush with slightly beaten egg and bake in moderate oven (375 ° F.) 15—20 min.

To shape *Cinnamon Buns*

Roll and fill remaining dough less ¹/₂ lb. and shape in roll as above. Cut roll into small buns. Place on buttered baking sheets and allow to rise. Brush with slightly beaten egg, sprinkle with sugar and bake in moderately hot oven (425 ° F.) 5—10 min. For different shapes, see illustration. Use remaining ¹/₂ lb. dough for Granny's Coffee Rings, next page.

To shape *Granny's Coffee Rings* (50 cookies)

$^1/_2$ lb. dough   *Garnish:*

$^1/_2$ cup butter   pearl sugar

$^1/_3$ cup cream

$1^1/_2$ cups flour

Add butter and cream to dough and work well. Then add flour to make dough firm and smooth. Divide into 5 equal portions and roll out portions well in thin lengths of finger thickness. Shape rings and dip in pearl sugar. Bake in moderate oven (375 ° F.) 10 min. or until light brown. Allow to cool on baking sheet. Dry in very slow oven. Cookies should be very brittle.

Coffee Cake   *Kaffekaka i form*

3 cups flour	1 cup lukewarm cream
$^1/_2$ cup butter	1 egg
1 yeast cake	$^1/_2$ cup seedless raisins
5 tablespoons sugar	3 tablespoons almonds,
$^1/_4$ teaspoon salt	chopped

Mix yeast with 1 tablespoon sugar. Sift flour into large bowl; dot with butter, add cream, yeast, sugar, salt, egg and raisins. Beat with wooden spoon until smooth and firm. Place in well buttered baking dish, cover and allow to rise. Brush with slightly beaten egg. Sprinkle with sugar and chopped almonds and bake in slow to moderate oven (325 ° F.) 20 min. Serve warm in rectangular pieces.

Swedish Pastry   *Wienerbröd*

$1^1/_2$ cups butter   *Filling:*

$3^3/_4$ cups flour   Apple Sauce, Almond Paste or

$1^1/_4$ cups milk   Vanilla Cream (see below)

$1^1/_2$ yeast cakes

$^1/_4$ cup sugar

1 egg

Sift $^1/_3$ cup flour onto baking board. Cut butter into flour with 2 knives or pastry mixer. Let stand in cold place.

Mix yeast with 1 tablespoon sugar. Add cold milk, egg and sugar.

Swedish Pastry different shapes (Crescents, Envelopes, Combs).

Add flour gradually and beat with wooden spoon until smooth and glossy. Roll out on well floured baking board to 14″ × 14″ square. Roll out butter dough to 6″ × 12″ rectangle, place on other dough and fold over other half of latter. Roll out and fold in 3 parts from left to right, as though folding napkin, 3 times. Leave in cold place ¹/₂ hr.

To shape *Envelopes*

Roll out dough thin and cut in 4″×4″ squares. Spread with 1 table-spoon filling. Fold corners in toward center and press down edges.

To shape *Cocks' Combs*

Roll out dough thin and cut in strips 5″ wide. Place filling in middle and fold both sides over. Turn onto pearl sugar and chopped almonds. Cut in pieces 4″ long and gash one side 5 times.

To shape *Crescents*

Roll out dough thin and cut in strips 5″ wide. Cut in triangles 3″ wide at base. Place filling on base and roll up.

Place pastry on buttered baking sheet and leave in cold place to rise. Brush Envelopes and Crescents with slightly beaten egg. Bake in hot oven (450 ° F.) until golden yellow. When cold, spread Envelopes and Crescents with icing made of confectioner's sugar and water.

Fillings:

Almond Paste	¹/₂ cup sugar
¹/₄ lb. almonds	1 egg

Grind blanched almonds and mix with sugar. Add egg gradually and work until smooth.

Vanilla Cream	1 egg yolk
¹/₂ cup milk	1 tablespoon sugar
1 tablespoon flour	¹/₂ teaspoon vanilla extract

Mix all ingredients except vanilla in double boiler. Cook over boiling water, stirring constantly, until thick. Cool, stirring occasionally, and add vanilla.

Saffron Bread   *Saffransbröd*

8 cups flour	1—1¹/₂ cups sugar
2¹/₂ cups lukewarm milk	¹/₄ teaspoon salt
2 yeast cakes	30 almonds, ground
1 egg	(4 bitter almonds, ground)
1 teaspoon saffron	1 cup seedless raisins
1 cup melted butter	

Mix yeast with 1 tablespoon sugar. Dry saffron in warm oven and pound smooth with small amount of sugar or dissolve in 1 table-spoon brandy. Mix milk, saffron, sugar, salt, egg, butter and small amount of flour. Add yeast and remaining flour; beat with wooden spoon until smooth and firm. Sprinkle with flour, cover with clean towel and let rise in warm place until doubled in bulk, about 2 hrs. Turn out on floured baking board and knead until smooth. Divide into portions and make braided loaves and buns in different shapes. See color illustration, page 112. Place on buttered baking sheets, cover and let rise. Brush with slightly beaten egg. Sprinkle with sugar and chopped almonds and bake loaves in moderately hot oven (375 ° F.) 15—20 min., buns in hot oven (425 ° F.) 5—10 min.

Rye Rusks   *Kryddskorpor*

2 cups rye flour and	$^1/_2$ cup butter
6 cups white flour,	$^1/_3$ cup sugar
or 8 cups white flour	$^1/_4$ teaspoon salt
$2^1/_2$ cups lukewarm milk	$^1/_2$ cup molasses
2 yeast cakes	3 orange peels
2 tablespoons fat	

Cook orange peels in water until soft. Shave off white part and chop remainder finely. Melt fat and butter in milk and pour into large bowl. Add molasses, sugar, salt, yeast mixed with small amount of sugar and orange peels. Then add flour gradually and beat until firm and smooth. Sprinkle dough with flour, cover with towel and let rise in warm place until doubled in bulk. Turn out onto floured baking board and knead well. Divide in 6 parts and roll out in long loaves. Place on buttered baking sheets. Let rise and bake in moderate oven (375 °F.) 15—20 min. Remove to towel, brush with warm water and cool. When cold, halve loaves lengthwise cut in slices 1 inch thick, and place on baking sheets and dry in slow oven until light brown.

Turn off heat, keeping oven door slightly open, and leave rusks until thoroughly dry and crisp. Illustration, page 114.

Round Rusks   *Brutna skorpor*

4 cups flour	$^1/_4$ teaspoon salt
$1^1/_4$ cups lukewarm milk	$^1/_4$ cup butter
2 tablespoons fat	$^1/_2$ cup sugar
1 yeast cake	

Continued on page 114.

Christmas Breads and Pastries

Lucia Ginger Snaps
Saffron Bread*
Ginger Cake
Christmas Crullers

Butter Leaves with Jelly
Brandy Rings
Almond Tarts

* in twists and old-fashioned shapes known as Christmas Waggons, Vicar's Hair, Lucia Rolls.

Cakes and Cookies

Top:
Polynées
Sunday Cake

Center:
Vanilla Cookies
Dream Cookies
Vanilla Rocks
Coffee Fingers
Torte with Vanilla Cream Filling

Lower Left Hand Corner:
Butter Leaves
Spritz Rings

Lower Right Hand Corner:
Oat Cookies
Diagonals
Almond Ginger Snaps

Lower Center:
Doughnuts

Melt fat and butter in lukewarm milk and pour into large bowl. Mix yeast cake with 1 tablespoon sugar and add with salt and sugar to milk. Then add flour gradually, beating hard, until dough is firm and glossy. Sprinkle dough with a little flour, cover with towel and allow to rise in warm place until doubled in bulk. Turn out onto floured baking board and knead. Divide into 3 pieces and roll in uniform loaves. Cut each loave into about 15 uniform pieces and roll each round and round until perfectly smooth on top. Place on greased baking sheets, cover with towel and let rise until light. Bake in moderately hot oven (425 ° F.) until light brown. Remove to towel and cool. When cold, break in halves, using fork. Place in baking pan and dry in slow oven until light brown.

Turn off heat, keeping oven door slightly open, and leave rusks until thoroughly dry and crisp.

Rusks are prepared for drying

Rye Bread   *Rågbröd*

6 cups rye flour
2 cups white flour
2¹/₂ cups milk
2 yeast cakes
1¹/₂ teaspoons salt

¹/₃ cup fat or butter
³/₄ cup molasses
2—3 teaspoons fennel seed or
aniseed, pounded

Mix yeast with 1 tablespoon sugar. Melt fat, add milk and heat until lukewarm. Pour into big bowl, add molasses and half of rye flour and mix well. Then add yeast, salt, seeds and remaining flour gradually. Beat well until smooth and firm, cover with towel and allow to rise in warm place until almost doubled in bulk. Turn out onto floured baking board and knead well. Divide in 6 pieces; roll each piece into round flat loaf. Cut out a hole in center. Place on buttered baking sheet, prick with fork, cover and let rise. Bake in hot oven (425 ° F.) 15 min. until light brown. Remove to towel, brush with warm water and cover with towel or cloth.

Shape into 3 loaves, prick with fork and let rise. Bake in moderate oven (375 ° F.) 30 min. Brush with warm water when half done and again when ready.

Christmas Bread (3 loaves)   *Vörtlimpor*

3 cups stout
3 yeast cakes
1 teaspoon salt
6 cups rye flour
3 cups white flour

1 cup molasses
¹/₄ cup fat or butter
4 orange peels, chopped
2 tablespoons aniseed or fennel
seed, pounded

Mix yeast with 1 tablespoon sugar. Melt fat, add stout and heat until lukewarm. Pour into large bowl, add molasses and half flour and mix well. Then add yeast, salt, orange peels, seeds and flour gradually, leaving one cup white flour. Beat well until dough is smooth and firm. Cover with towel and allow to rise in warm place until almost doubled in bulk. Turn onto floured baking board and knead with remaining flour until firm and glossy. Divide in 3 parts and shape in long loaves. Place on buttered baking sheet and cover with cloth. Leave to rise. Prick surfaces with toothpick and bake in slow oven (250 ° F.) 30—40 min. When half done, brush with water to which a little molasses has been added; brush again when done. Place between cloths to keep crust soft.

CAKES

Sunday Cake — *Sockerkaka*

1¹/₂ cups flour	3 eggs
2 teaspoons baking powder	1 cup sugar, scant
¹/₂ cup water	1 tablespoon lemon rind, grated
¹/₄ cup butter	

Sift flour and baking powder together. Bring water to boiling point, add butter and cool. Beat eggs with sugar until white and fluffy. Add flour, lemon rind and water. Stir until blended, then pour into well buttered and bread-crumbed deep round cake pan. Bake in slow oven (250° F.) 60 min.   See illustration, page 113.

Sand Cake — *Sandkaka*

1 cup butter, scant	³/₄ cup potato flour
³/₄ cup flour	3 eggs
2 teaspoons baking powder	2 tablespoons brandy
1 cup sugar, scant	

Melt butter and cool. Sift together flour and baking powder. Work butter, sugar and potato flour until white and fluffy. Add eggs and continue to beat. Add brandy and flour, stir until well blended and pour into well buttered and bread-crumbed deep round cake pan. Bake in slow oven (250° F.) 60 min.

Chocolate Cake — *Chokladkaka*

1¹/₄ cups flour	1 teaspoon vanilla extract
1 teaspoon baking powder	3 squares (3 oz.) sweet choco-
¹/₃ cup butter	late, melted,
³/₄ cup sugar	*or* 3 tablespoons cocoa
2 eggs	¹/₂ cup cream

Sift flour and baking powder together. Work butter, sugar and egg yolks until creamy. Add vanilla, melted chocolate (or cocoa) and cream alternately with flour. Fold in stiffly beaten egg whites. Pour into well buttered and bread-crumbed deep round cake pan and bake in slow oven (250° F.) 50 min.

Jelly Roll and
Chocolate Roll

Ginger Cake

Mjuk pepparkaka

¹/₂ cup butter

1 cup sugar

3 eggs

1 teaspoon cinnamon

1 teaspoon ginger

2 teaspoons cloves

1³/₄ cups flour

1 teaspoon baking soda

²/₃ cup sour cream

Work butter and sugar until white and fluffy; add eggs and spices.
Add flour and baking soda sifted together alternately with cream.
Stir until well blended. Pour into well buttered and bread-crumbed
deep round cake pan and bake in moderate oven (325 ° F.) 15 min.
Reduce heat to 250 ° F. and continue to bake 30 min. longer.   See
illustration, page 112.

Jelly Roll

Rulltårta

3 eggs

¹/₂ cup sugar

²/₃ cup flour

1 teaspoon baking powder

Filling:

jam or apple sauce

Sift flour and baking powder together. Beat eggs and sugar until
white and fluffy. Add flour, stirring until well blended. Pour into
oblong pan lined with buttered waxed paper. Bake in moderately hot
oven (425 ° F.) 5 min. Turn out on waxed paper sprinkled with sugar.
Remove bottom paper. Spread with jam or apple sauce. Roll lengthwise. Wrap in waxed paper. When cold, cut crosswise in slices.

Chocolate Roll   *Chokladrulltårta*

3 eggs	*Filling:*
3/4 cup sugar	1/2 cup butter
1/3 cup potato flour	1/2 cup powdered sugar
2 tablespoons cocoa	2 egg yolks
2 teaspoons baking powder	1 teaspoon vanilla extract

Beat eggs and sugar until white and fluffy. Sift together flour, cocoa and baking powder. Add and stir in until well blended. Pour batter into oblong pan lined with buttered waxed paper. Bake in moderately hot oven (425° F.) 5 min. Turn onto waxed paper sprinkled with sugar and leave until cold.

Filling: Work butter and sugar until fluffy. Stir in egg yolks and vanilla extract. Spread cake with filling, roll up lengthwise. Wrap in waxed paper. Leave some hours, then cut crosswise in slices. Illustration, page 117.

Torte with Vanilla Cream Filling   *Sockerkakstårta med vaniljkräm*

4 eggs	3/4 tablespoon potato flour
3/4 cup sugar	1 cup cream
1 teaspoon baking powder	1 teaspoon vanilla extract
1/3 cup flour	2 tablespoons sugar
1/3 cup potato flour	*Icing:*
Filling:	1 cup powdered sugar
2 egg yolks	1 1/2 tablespoons water
1 1/2 tablespoons butter	1/2 tablespoon lemon juice

Sift flour with potato flour and baking powder. Beat egg whites until stiff. Add sugar, egg yolks and flour. Pour into well buttered and bread-crumbed deep round cake pan or iron frying pan and bake in moderate oven (350° F.) 30 min.

Filling: Mix all ingredients except vanilla extract in double boiler and cook until smooth and thick, stirring constantly. Remove from heat, add vanilla extract and beat occasionally until cold.

Mix all ingredients of icing and stir until smooth.

When cold cut cake into 2—3 layers. Spread each layer with filling and cover top evenly with icing. Decorate with jam. (See illustration.)

Torte garnished with Icing and Jam

Thousand Leaves Torte

Squares are marked with special icing (¹/₂ cup confectioners' sugar and ¹/₂ egg white beaten together until smooth) forced through fine paper tube.

Whipped cream may be substituted for icing.

Ambrosia Cake

Ambrosiakaka

2 eggs	*Icing:*
²/₃ cup sugar, scant	1 tablespoon orange juice
²/₃ cup butter	¹/₃ cup powdered sugar
²/₃ cup flour	3 tablespoons candied orange
¹/₂ teaspoon baking powder	peel, chopped, or chopped
	almonds

Beat eggs and sugar until white and fluffy. Work butter until creamy and add. Sift together flour and baking powder and stir in until well blended. Pour into well buttered and bread-crumbed cake pan and bake in slow oven (250 ° F.) 30 min.

Icing: Stir sugar and orange juice until smooth. Spread evenly over cake and sprinkle with orange peel or finely chopped almonds.

Opera Torte

Operatårta

4 eggs	¹/₂ tablespoon gelatine
²/₃ cup sugar	¹/₂ teaspoon vanilla extract
1 tablespoon flour	
4 tablespoons potato flour	1 cup whipped cream
Cream Filling:	*Almond Paste:*
2 egg yolks	1 cup blanched almonds
1 tablespoon sugar	²/₃ cup powdered sugar
2 teaspoons potato flour	1 egg white
1 cup cream	green coloring

Mix 3 egg yolks with one egg, add sugar and beat until white and fluffy. Sift flour and potato flour together and add to mixture. Beat remaining egg whites stiff; fold in carefully. Pour batter in well buttered and bread-crumbed deep round cake pan or iron frying pan and bake in slow oven (350 ° F.) 30 min.

Filling: Soak gelatine in small amount cold water. Mix egg yolks, sugar, potato flour and cream in double boiler and cook gently until smooth and thick, stirring constantly. Remove from heat, add gelatine and vanilla and beat occasionally until cold. Fold in whipped cream.

Ambrosia
Cake, Uppåkra
Cookies,
AlmondRusks,
Rye Cookies,
and Meringues

Opera Torte,
Cream Puffs,
Almond Wa-
fers, and
Almond Rings

Put almonds through grinder twice. Work with sugar and egg
white 10 min. or until smooth. Roll out on wax paper; shape in
large circle.

Divide cake in three layers. Spread filling between layers and on
top of cake, cover with Almond Paste and sprinkle with powdered
sugar. Put in refrigerator until serving time.

Preparing
Thousand
Leaves Torte;
Torte
garnished,
page 119

Thousand Leaves Torte   *Tusenbladstårta*

1 cup cold unsalted butter
1²/₃ cups flour
4 tablespoons ice water
Filling:
apple sauce
Vanilla Cream Filling (page 118)
Icing:
1 cup powdered sugar

1¹/₂ tablespoons water
¹/₂ tablespoon lemon juice
Garnish:
1 cup heavy cream, whipped
  with 1 teaspoon sugar
candied orange peels, cut in
  strips
almonds

Sift flour on baking board. Cut in butter with 2 knives or pastry mixer. Turn into bowl, add ice water gradually and work with wooden spoon until smooth. Cover and chill ¹/₂ hr. Divide into 6 or 7 portions. Roll out each very thinly on wax paper, cut out circle and prick with fork. Place circles with wax paper underneath on baking sheets. Brush with ice water, sprinkle with sugar and bake in hot oven (450° F.) 6—8 min. until golden brown. Keep on wax paper until cold.

Spread layers alternately with apple sauce and Vanilla Cream Filling. Spread top with icing. Garnish with candied orange peels, almonds and whipped cream forced through pastry tube.

Mazarin Torte and
Individual Mazarins

Mazarin Torte   *Mazarintårta*

$^{1}/_{2}$ cup unsalted butter $^{1}/_{3}$ cup butter
$^{1}/_{4}$ cup powdered sugar $^{2}/_{3}$ cup blanched almonds,
1 egg yolk   ground
1 cup flour   2 eggs
Filling: (green coloring)
$^{1}/_{2}$ cup sugar

Work butter and sugar until white and fluffy. Add egg yolk and flour
and stir until smooth. Leave dough in refrigerator one hour.

Filling: Work sugar and butter until smooth. Add almonds, eggs
(and green coloring) and mix until well blended.

Roll out dough, line well buttered pie tin and spread filling
evenly. Bake in slow oven (250° F.) 30 min. Cool in tin. Sprinkle
with powdered sugar or cover with icing ($^{1}/_{2}$ cup powdered sugar
mixed with 1 tablespoon water).

Mazarins   *Mazariner*

Proceed as above but bake in small individual tart shells in moderate
oven (375° F.) 20 min. Top with icing or powdered sugar.

COOKIES

Almond Ginger Snaps

Skurna pepparkakor

1 cup butter	2 teaspoons cloves
1 cup sugar	1 teaspoon baking soda
1/2 cup molasses	3 1/2 cups flour
1 tablespoon ginger	1 cup blanched almonds
2 teaspoons cinnamon	

Work butter until creamy. Add sugar, molasses, spices, baking soda, almonds and flour. Turn onto floured baking board and knead until smooth. Shape into 2 thick, slightly flattened rolls. Wrap each in wax paper and chill thoroughly. Cut crosswise with sharp knife in thin slices. Place on greased baking sheet and bake in moderate oven (325 ° F.) 8—10 min.

Ginger Snaps

Pepparkakor

2/3 cup brown or ordinary sugar	3/4 tablespoon baking soda
2/3 cup molasses	2/3 cup butter
1 teaspoon ginger	1 egg
1 teaspoon cinnamon	5 cups flour
1/2 teaspoon cloves	

Heat sugar, molasses and spices to boiling point. Add baking soda and pour mixture over butter in bowl. Stir until butter melts. Add egg and sifted flour and blend thoroughly. Knead on baking board. Chill. Roll out and cut with fancy cutters (at Christmas into Santa Claus shapes, Christmas trees, hearts, animal forms etc.). Place on greased baking sheet and bake in slow to moderate oven (325 ° F.) 8—10 min.

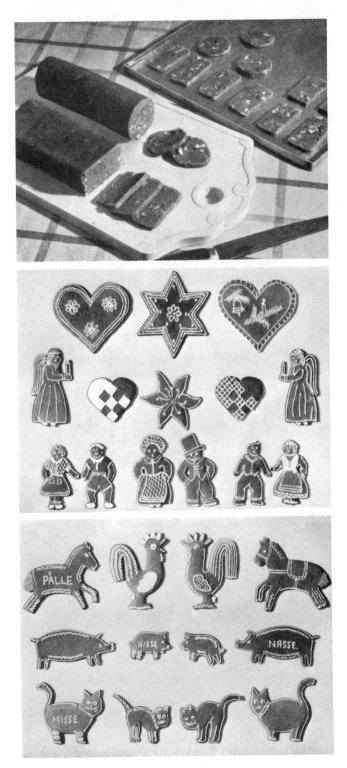

Preparing Almond
Ginger Snaps

Christmas
Ginger Snaps

Christmas
Ginger Snaps

Lucia Ginger Snaps   *Luciapepparkakor*

1¹/₂ cups heavy cream	1 tablespoon lemon rind, grated
2¹/₂ cups brown sugar	2 tablespoons baking soda
1¹/₄ cups molasses	9 cups flour
1 tablespoon ginger	

Whip cream, add sugar, molasses, ginger, lemon rind and baking soda and stir 10 min. Add flour and work until smooth. Cover and leave in cool place overnight. Turn onto floured baking board and roll out thin. With floured cutters, cut out Santa Claus shapes, gingerbread men, houses, animals or other desired figures. Brush with water and bake on greased cookie sheet in slow oven (250 ° F.) 15 min. Leave on sheet to cool.

To make house, cut out paper pattern. Roll out dough on greased baking sheet, lay pattern over and cut around, using sharp knife. Bake as above. When cold, join pieces together by dipping edges in sugar melted in saucepan. Decorate with icing (¹/₂ cup confectioners' sugar and ¹/₂ egg white beaten together until smooth) forced through fine paper tube.

Swedish Puff Paste   *Smördeg*

1 cup cold unsalted butter

1²/₃ cups flour

4 tablespoons ice water

Sift flour onto baking board. Cut in butter with 2 knives or pastry mixer. Add ice water gradually and work until blended. Chill 30 min. Roll out on floured baking board to rectangular shape, fold and repeat 2 or 3 times, chilling 30 min. each time. Then roll out quickly to desired thickness and cut in different shapes (see below). Place on baking sheet rinsed in cold water and keep in cold place 10—15 min. before baking. Brush with water or beaten egg and bake in very hot oven (475 ° F.) 8—10 min. Reduce heat when golden yellow.

Christmas Gingerbread Houses

Folding Christmas Stars

Folding Envelopes

Butter Rings

To shape *Christmas Stars*   *Julstjärnor*

Cut 4″ squares. Place teaspoon jam in middle of each. Cut each corner $1^1/2''$ toward center, fold alternate corners in and press edges together. Brush with beaten egg and bake.

To shape *Envelopes*   *Konvolut*

Cut 4″ squares. Place jam in centers and fold dough over. Brush with beaten egg and bake.

To shape *Butter Rings*   *Smörkransar*

Cut dough in rings 2″ in diameter. Brush with water; sprinkle with sugar and chopped almonds. Bake.

128

Butter Leaves (80 cookies) *Mörkakor*

1 cup unsalted butter
$^{1}/_{2}$ cup sugar
1 egg yolk
4 blanched bitter almonds, grated
$2^{1}/_{2}$ cups flour

Garnish:
1 egg white
25 almonds, chopped
4 tablespoons sugar

Work butter and sugar until creamy and fluffy. Add egg yolk, bitter almonds and flour and mix thoroughly. Chill. Roll out thin on floured baking board and cut in shapes with cookie cutter. Brush with beaten egg white and sprinkle with mixed almonds and sugar. Place on buttered baking sheet and bake in moderate oven (350° F.) 8—10 min. or until golden yellow. See illustration, page 113.

Butter Leaves with Jelly (40 cookies) *Syltkakor*

Prepare dough as in recipe above. Roll dough out thin and cut in round cakes. Cut hole in half of cakes, brush with egg white and sprinkle with almond and sugar. Place all cookies on buttered baking sheet and bake. Put together two and two with jam between. See illustration, page 112.

Coffee Fingers (55 cookies) *Mördegspinnar*

1 cup unsalted butter
$^{1}/_{4}$ cup sugar
6 bitter almonds, grated
$2^{1}/_{2}$ cups flour

Garnish:
1 egg
15 blanched almonds, finely chopped
2 tablespoons sugar

Work butter and sugar until creamy and fluffy. Add bitter almonds and flour and mix thoroughly. Chill. Roll out to finger thickness; cut in 2″ strips. Brush with beaten egg; sprinkle with mixed sugar and almonds. Bake in moderate oven (350° F.) 8—10 min. or until golden yellow. See illustration, page 113.

Uppåkra Cookies (50 cookies) *Uppåkrakakor*

1 cup unsalted butter
$^{1}/_{3}$ cup sugar
$^{3}/_{4}$ cup potato flour
$1^{3}/_{4}$ cups flour

Garnish:
1 egg
$^{1}/_{3}$ cup blanched almonds, chopped
3 tablespoons pearl sugar

Work butter and sugar until creamy and fluffy. Add potato flour, then ordinary flour and mix thoroughly. Chill. Roll out thin on floured baking board and cut in rounds 2" in diameter. Fold over almost in middle, brush with beaten egg and sprinkle with mixed sugar and almonds. Place on buttered baking sheet and bake in moderate oven (350 ° F.) 10 min. or until golden yellow. Illustration, page 121.

Rye Cookies (50 cookies) *Rågkakor*

1 cup unsalted butter	1¹/₄ cups rye flour
¹/₃ cup sugar	1¹/₄ cups white flour

Work butter and sugar until creamy and fluffy. Add flour and mix thoroughly. Chill. Turn onto floured baking board; roll out thin. Prick surface with fork and cut rounds with floured cutter 2¹/₂" in diameter. Cut round holes as shown in illustration page 121. Place on buttered baking sheet and bake in moderate oven (350 ° F.) until golden yellow (about 10 min.).

Brandy Rings (75 cookies) *Konjakskransar*

1¹/₃ cups unsalted butter	3¹/₂ cups flour
³/₄ cup sugar	3 tablespoons brandy

Mix all ingredients and work until smooth. Turn onto floured baking board and roll into thin lengths, twist 2 and 2 together like twine, cut in 4—5" pieces and shape in rings. Place on buttered baking sheet and bake in moderate oven (350 ° F.) until golden yellow (about 10 min.).   See illustration, page 112.

Diagonals (40 cookies) *Spårkakor*

1 cup unsalted butter	2¹/₂ cups flour
¹/₂ cup sugar	currant jelly
1 egg yolk	

Work butter and sugar until creamy and fluffy. Add egg yolk and flour, mix thoroughly and cool. Then roll out ¹/₃ of dough into 2 strips about 2—2¹/₂" wide and place on well buttered baking sheet. Force remaining dough through pastry tube, making three rows on each strip. Bake in moderate oven (350° F.) until golden yellow (about 10 min.). When strips are cold, force currant jelly through small paper funnel between rows and cut into 1″ diagonals. See illustration, page 113.

Spritz Rings (40—50 cookies)   *Spritsar*

1 cup unsalted butter	6 blanched bitter almonds,
1/2 cup sugar	grated
1 egg yolk	2 1/2 cups flour

Work butter and sugar until creamy and fluffy. Add egg yolk, almonds, flour and mix thoroughly. Shape in rings or S's with cookie press. Place on buttered baking sheet and bake in moderate oven (350° F.) until golden yellow (about 8 min.). See illustration, page 113.

Oat Cookies (50 cookies)   *Havrekakor*

3 cups oatmeal
2/3 cup butter
1/2 cup sugar

Mix ingredients on baking board; knead until well blended. Roll dough out into small balls and flatten crosswise with fork. Place on buttered baking sheet and bake in slow to moderate oven (325 ° F.) until light brown (about 8 min.). See illustration, page 113.

Dream Cookies (70 cookies)   *Drömmar*

1 cup unsalted butter	1 teaspoon baking powder
3/4 cup sugar	2 cups flour
2 teaspoons vanilla extract	35 blanched almonds

Brown butter slightly and pour into bowl. Place over cold water and cool. Add sugar and stir until fluffy. Add vanilla, then flour and baking powder sifted together. Work dough until smooth. Roll out into small balls. Place on buttered baking sheet with half almond on top of each. Bake in slow oven (250° F.) until golden brown (about 30 min.). See illustration, page 113.

131

Vanilla Cookies (60—70 cookies)   *Brysselkäx*

1 cup unsalted butter   2^1/$_2$ cups flour
^{1}/$_4$ cup sugar   2 teaspoons vanilla extract

Work butter and sugar until creamy and fluffy. Add flour and vanilla extract and mix thoroughly. Shape in roll 1^1/$_2$" in diameter. Roll in sugar mixed with cocoa and wrap in wax paper. Chill in refrigerator. Slice crosswise, place on buttered baking sheets and bake in moderate oven (350° F.) until golden yellow (about 8 min.).

Variation: Divide dough in 2 portions. Add 1 tablespoon cocoa to 1 portion and work until well blended. Shape each into 2 rolls, then make 1 long thick roll of all 4 (see illustration). Wrap in wax paper and chill in refrigerator. Slice crosswise, place on buttered baking sheets and bake in moderate oven (350° F.) until golden yellow (about 8 min.).   See illustration, page 113.

Vanilla Rocks (50 cookies)   *Vaniljkakor*

1 cup butter   2^1/$_2$ cups flour
^{1}/$_2$ cup powdered sugar   2 teaspoons vanilla extract
1 egg yolk

Work butter and sugar until creamy and fluffy, add egg yolk and flour and mix thoroughly. Force dough in tops through broad pastry tube onto well buttered baking sheet. Bake in moderate oven (350° F.) until golden yellow (about 8 min.). When cold, garnish center with jelly or sprinkle with powdered sugar.   See illustration, page 113.

Almond Tarts (35 tarts)   *Mandelformar*

^{2}/$_3$ cup unsalted butter   2—3 blanched bitter almonds,
^{1}/$_3$ cup sugar   grated
1 egg yolk   1^1/$_2$ cups flour
^{1}/$_2$ cup blanched almonds,
    grated

Work butter and sugar until creamy and fluffy. Add egg yolk, almonds and flour and mix thoroughly. Chill. Butter small fluted tins and with floured thumbs coat inside with dough. Bake in slow to moderate oven (325 ° F.) until light brown (about 10 min.). Allow to cool in tins, then unmold. Serve plain or fill with jam and whipped cream.   See illustration, page 112.

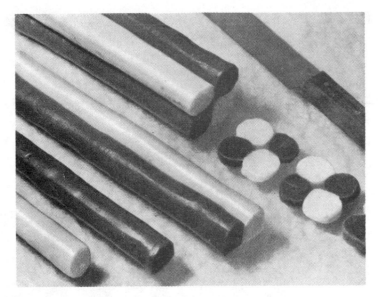

Slicing Vanilla Cookies

Almond Tarts

Filling and covering Custard Tarts

Custard Tarts (20 tarts)   *Linser*

$^3/_4$ cup unsalted butter
$^1/_3$ cup sugar
2 egg yolks
2 cups flour

Filling:
2 egg yolks
1 tablespoon potato flour
2 tablespoons sugar
$1^1/_4$ cups cream
vanilla extract

Work butter and sugar until creamy. Add egg yolks and flour and work until smooth. Chill.

Mix all ingredients for filling in double boiler and cook gently until smooth and thick, stirring constantly. Add vanilla extract to taste. Cool, stirring occasionally.

Butter individual tins and line with dough. Pour a little filling in each. Roll out remaining dough, cover tops, press edges and cut. Bake in slow to moderate oven (325 ° F.) 20 min. Allow to cool in tins. Unmold and sprinkle with powdered sugar.

Polynées (30 tarts)   *Polynéer*

3/4 cup unsalted butter	*Filling:*
1/3 cup sugar	1 cup almonds, ground
2 egg yolks	1 1/2 cups powdered sugar
2 cups flour	4 egg whites

Work butter and sugar until creamy. Add egg yolks and flour, working until smooth. Chill.

Filling: Mix almonds, sugar and egg whites and beat until smooth and fluffy (about 15 min.).

Roll out dough. Butter individual fluted cake tins, then line with greater part of dough and fill 3/4 with filling. Roll out remainder of dough, cut in strips and arrange in cross on top. Press edges. Bake in slow to moderate oven (325 ° F.) until golden yellow (about 20 min.). See illustration, page 113.

Almond Wafers (50 cookies)   *Flarn*

2/3 cup blanched almonds	1 tablespoon flour
1/2 cup sugar	2 tablespoons milk
1/2 cup butter	

Grind almonds and mix with other ingredients in skillet, stirring until butter melts. Drop teaspoonfuls of mixture about 4″ apart on well greased and floured cookie sheet. Bake in moderate oven (350 ° F.) until light brown (8—10 min.). Allow to cool slightly and then lay over rolling pin to shape. Illustration, page 121.

Almond Rusks (50 cookies)   *Mandelskorpor*

2 eggs	1 teaspoon baking powder
3/4 cup sugar	1 1/2 cups flour
2/3 cup almonds, chopped	

Beat eggs and sugar until white and fluffy. Add almonds and flour and baking powder sifted together and stir until well blended. Pour mixture onto well greased baking sheets in two 1 1/2″ wide rows. Bake in moderate oven (350 ° F.) 10 min. When done, cut in 1/2″ slices. Separate slices and return to slow oven (250 ° F.) 8 min. Turn off heat and leave in oven to dry (about 20 min.). Illustration, page 121.

Swedish Macaroons

Swedish Macaroons — *Konfektbröd*

1¹/₃ cups blanched almonds, ground   1¹/₂ cups powdered sugar
    1¹/₂—2 egg whites

Put almonds through grinder twice, second time with sugar. Work mixture until smooth and firm, adding egg whites gradually. Drop teaspoonfuls on well greased and floured cookie sheets or force mixture through fluted pastry tube in various shapes (see illustration). Decorate with strips of candied orange peel, cherries and nuts. Bake in slow to moderate oven (325 ° F.) until light yellow (about 30 min.).

Walnut Meringues (20—25 meringues) — *Valnötmaränger*

4 egg whites
1¹/₂ cups powdered sugar
1 cup walnuts, chopped

Mix egg whites and sugar in bowl. Bring water almost to boiling point but do not allow to boil. Place bowl over water and beat mixture vigorously 20 min. Chop walnuts coarsely; fold in carefully. Drop teaspoonfuls of mixture on well greased baking sheet and bake in very slow oven (200 ° F.) until light yellow (about 30 min.). Illustration, page 121.

Cream Puffs (12 puffs) *Petits choux*

²/₃ cup water
1 teaspoon sugar
¹/₃ cup butter

²/₃ cup flour
2 eggs

Heat butter, water and sugar to boiling point. Remove from heat. Add flour and stir vigorously until mixture is smooth and leaves sides of pan. Add eggs one by one, beating after each addition. When all ingredients are added, beat 10—15 min. Drop by tablespoonfuls on buttered baking sheet, or use pastry bag and tube. Bake in slow to moderate oven (325 ° F.) until firm and golden yellow (about 20 min.). If removed from oven too soon, cream puffs will fall. Cool, then slit tops and fill with whipped cream or ice cream. Serve immediately. Illustration, page 121.

Almond Rings (18—20 tarts) *Mandelkransar*

1 cup unsalted butter
¹/₃ cup sugar
2 egg yolks
25 blanched almonds, ground
2—3 blanched bitter almonds, ground

1¹/₃ cups flour
40—50 blanched almonds, chopped

Butter small fluted ring-shaped tins and sprinkle with chopped almonds. Work butter and sugar until creamy. Add egg yolks, ground almonds and sifted flour and mix thoroughly. Spread evenly in tins and bake in slow to moderate oven (325 ° F.) 20 min. Allow to cool in tins. Illustration, page 121.

Doughnuts (35 doughnuts) *Flottyrkransar*

1¹/₂ cups flour
1 teaspoon baking powder
1 egg
¹/₃ cup sugar
¹/₃ cup cream
2 tablespoons melted butter

¹/₂ tablespoon lemon rind, grated
or 5 cardamon seeds, pounded
To fry:
deep fat

Beat egg and sugar in bowl, add flour and baking powder sifted together, then add cream, butter and lemon rind or cardamom. Mix well and chill. Turn onto floured baking board and roll out to $^1/_8''$ thickness. Cut out rings with round cookie cutter with small hole in center. Fry in deep fat (375 ° F.) until golden brown and drain on absorbent paper. Turn in sugar and serve hot with jam as dessert or cold with coffee. See illustration, page 113.

Christmas Crullers (50 cookies) *Klenäter*

4 egg yolks	1 tablespoon brandy
$^1/_4$ cup powdered sugar	1 tablespoon lemon rind, grated
3 tablespoons butter	*To fry:*
$1^1/_2$ cups flour	deep fat

Mix ingredients and stir until well blended. Chill. Turn dough onto floured baking board. Roll out thin. With pastry wheel, cut strips $^3/_4''$ wide and 3'' long. Cut gash in center and twist end through. (See illustration, page 139.) Fry in deep fat (375 ° F.) until light brown. Drain on absorbent paper. Crullers are a typical Christmas delicacy, served with jam as dessert or with coffee. See illustration, page 112.

Rosettes (20 rosettes) *Sockerstruvor*

2 eggs	$^2/_3$ cup heavy cream
1 egg yolk	*To fry:*
$^1/_3$ cup sugar	deep fat
1 cup flour	

Beat eggs, egg yolk and cream together. Add flour and sugar. Stir until well blended. Let stand 2 hrs.

Put rosette iron in cold fat to cover. Heat fat to 375 ° F., remove iron, drain on absorbent paper and dip into well stirred batter. Hold coated iron over hot fat for a moment before dipping in. Cook until golden brown. Remove, slip rosette carefully from iron and drain on absorbent paper. Heat iron again and repeat. Sprinkle rosettes with sugar.

Christmas Crullers

Frying Rosettes in Deep Fat

MISCELLANEOUS

Striped Candies *Polkagrisar*

1 lb. sugar	2 teaspoons vinegar
1 cup water	3 drops peppermint oil
1 tablespoon dextrose	red coloring

Mix sugar, dextrose, water and vinegar in saucepan and let stand until dissolved. Bring quickly to boil and cook over low heat (275 ° F.) or until mixture becomes brittle when dropped in cold water. Remove from heat and allow to cool 3—4 min. Pour $^3/_4$ onto oiled baking sheet. Add peppermint and turn edges constantly towards middle with spatula. When cold enough to handle, stretch with oiled hands. Fold, stretch and fold continuously. Then pull into 1 long strip and place on oiled baking sheet. Color remaining candy red and pour onto baking sheet in 2 strips, one on either side of white candy. Twist strips together and cut immediately with oiled scissors into different shapes.

Molasses Candies *Knäck*

1 cup sugar	1 cup heavy cream
1 cup molasses	$^1/_3$ cup blanched almonds,
$^1/_4$ cup butter	coarsely chopped

Mix sugar, molasses, butter and cream in skillet. Cook over low heat (250 ° F.), stirring constantly, until mixture forms soft balls when dropped in cold water. Add almonds and pour in small fluted paper candy cups. Allow to set.

Striped Candies

Molasses Candies

Swedish Toffee

Swedish Toffee

Chokladkola

2³/₄ cups sugar
1¹/₄ cups molasses
2 tablespoons cocoa

3 tablespoons butter
2¹/₄ cups cream

Mix all ingredients and cook over slow heat (250 ° F.), stirring occasionally, until mixture forms soft balls when dropped in cold water. Pour into oiled oblong pan. Cool slightly and cut in small squares with oiled knife. Wrap in waxed paper. Illustration, page 141.

Christmas Wine

Julglögg

1 bottle (1 liter) aquavite
   (45 percent alcohol)
1 bottle Claret or red wine
10 cardamoms
5 cloves
3 bitter orange peels

4 figs
1 cup blanched almonds
1 cup raisins
1¹/₂ inch cinnamon stick
¹/₂ lb. lump sugar

Pour spirits into kettle. Add remaining ingredients except sugar lumps, cover and heat slowly to boiling point. Remove from heat. Put sugar on iron grill and place over kettle. Then put match to "glögg" and keep pouring burning "glögg" over sugar until melted. Remove grill and cover kettle. Cool. Keep in well corked bottles. Heat before serving but do not boil.

Serve hot in wine glasses with raisins and almonds.

Traditional Party and Everyday Menus

The following menus suggest ways of using the various recipes in this book. Particularly on holidays and special occasions, definite culinary traditions are followed. But there are also eating customs which prescribe that certain dishes be served on certain days or with certain other dishes. For example, Pea Soup with Pork followed by Pancakes with Jam is the standard Thursday dinner menu during the winter. Black Soup almost always precedes Goose, Brown Beans are associated with Fried Side Pork, and White Cabbage Soup is inseparable from Veal Meatballs. Nettle Soup, Salmon and Poached Eggs, Fried Chicken with Green Salad, and Ice Cream with Strawberries form the classic Swedish spring dinner. Use this chapter for hints when you want to give an authentic Swedish party or surprise your family with a Swedish meal.

Smörgåsbord Suggestions

For further Smörgåsbord suggestions, see pages 11 and 24.

Pickled Herring, Boiled Potatoes
Herring Salad
Anchovy au Gratin
Smoked Eel
Smoked Salmon
Pickled Fried Sardines or Smelts
Liver Sausage
Creamed Sweetbreads and Mushrooms in Pastry
    Shells
Stuffed Onions
Omelets with different fillings
Meatballs
Chicken Salad
Lobster in Aspic
Vegetable Salad in Mayonnaise
Tomatoes, Radishes, Celery
Pickled Fresh Cucumber
Cheese

Chef's Pickled Herring
Smoked Eel
Omelet with Creamed Mushrooms
Meatballs
Radishes, Tomatoes, Pickled Fresh Cucumber
Cheese

Pickled Herring
Sardines
Eggs and Caviar
Baked Fresh Sardines or Smelts
Sliced Ox Tongue or Ham
Potato Salad
Radishes, Tomatoes
Cheese

Dinner Menus

Smörgåsbord, Canapés or Bread, Butter, Herring and Cheese may be served as hors d'œuvre to all meals.

Nettle Soup with Egg Sections

Boiled Salmon, Hollandaise Sauce, Boiled New Potatoes and Dill

Roast Leg of Lamb, Browned Potatoes, Cauliflower, String Beans

Lemon Fromage

Clear Consommé with Vegetables

Smoked Salmon, Buttered Spinach, Poached Eggs

Fried Chicken, Browned Potatoes, Mixed Green Salad

Strawberries and Cream

Consommé with Asparagus tips

Rolled Fish Fillets with Lobster Sauce

Roasted Spareribs, Browned Potatoes, Apple Sauce and Prunes

Opera Torte

Vegetable Soup with Cheese Sandwiches

Beef Tongue with Mushroom Sauce, Mashed Potatoes and Peas

Chocolate Pudding

Royal Pot Roast, Browned Potatoes, Whole Fried Onions, Peas, Tomatoes

Apple Cake with Vanilla Sauce

Pot Roasted Veal, Browned Potatoes, String Beans, Carrots, Pickled Cucumber

Caramel Pudding

Baked Pike with Boiled Potatoes, Mixed Green Salad

Apple Dumplings with Vanilla Sauce

Beefsteak with Onions, Fried Potatoes

Clabbered Milk with Ginger Cookies

Fried Side Pork, Brown Beans

Mixed Fruit Soup

Filled Cabbage Rolls, Boiled Potatoes

Stewed Fruit

Pea Soup with Pork

Pancakes with Jam

Meatballs, Potatoes, Creamed Carrots, Pickled Cucumber

Rhubarb Cream with Milk

Sailors' Beef

Hip Soup with Whipped Cream and Almond
Rusks

White Cabbage Soup, Veal Meatballs

Rice Pudding, Fruit Syrup Sauce

Boiled Lamb with Dill Sauce, Potatoes and Green
Salad

Vanilla Ice Cream

Easter Eve Supper

The high point of Easter Eve is late supper, the main object of
which is to eat eggs. The table is spread with a white cloth decorated
with narcissi, the traditional birch switches with their tiny fresh
green leaves, yellow runners and toy chickens. The food consists of
eggs prepared in various ways and one or more hot dishes. In
order to celebrate Easter properly, even those who never eat eggs
at any other time try to manage at least one. The children compete
to see who can eat most dyed eggs. The following dishes make a
good Easter supper.

Bread, Butter, Cheese
Herring, Anchovies
Liver Paté and Pickled Fresh Cucumber
Boiled Sliced Ham
Eggs with Mayonnaise and Shrimps
Stuffed Eggs
Boiled Dyed Eggs
Omelet with Creamed Lobster
Kidney Sauté

Fried Sweetbreads and Peas

Mazarine Torte

In the course of the evening, an egg-toddy is often served. To make
it, egg yolks and sugar are stirred together until light and a few
teaspoons of cognac are added. Stirring egg-toddy can be made
an amusing game in which all compete to see who stirs best.

Crayfish Party

August is the month of crayfish and beautiful moonlight. Catching crayfish with nets, a popular sport, is permitted from the midnight between August 7 and 8 till the end of September, and the first crayfish parties are given on the evening of August 8. Colored paper lanterns are hung in the garden and if one is lucky the whole scene is illuminated by an August full moon. The table is decorated with candles and red paper ornaments, see illustration on page 48. Here are two menus for crayfish suppers.

Bread, Butter, Toast, Cheese
Chef's Pickled Herring
Canned Herring
Boiled Sliced Ham
Liver Paté and Pickled Fresh Cucumber
Vegetable Salad in Mayonnaise
Herring au Gratin
Baked Omelet with Creamed Mushrooms
Kidney Sauté
Small Meatballs

Crayfish

Torte with Vanilla Cream Filling

Fruit

Butter, Toast, Cheese

Crayfish

Roast Duck, Browned Potatoes, Peas, Green Salad
Apple Sauce

Raspberry Parfait.

An old custom, now fortunately falling into disuse, requires that every crayfish tail be rinsed down with a glass of brännvin.

Christmas Eve Supper

The climax of the Christmas celebrations in Sweden comes on Christmas Eve, when an especially prepared meal consisting of some of the following traditional dishes is served.

Sliced Christmas Bread and other kinds of bread, Butter, Cheese

Pickled Herring, Anchovies

Herring Salad

Head Cheese, Jellied Veal and Pork with Pickled Beets

Liver Paté and Pickled Gherkin

Sausages, boiled and smoked, hot and cold

Pigs' Head and Pigs' Feet

Christmas Ham with Mustard

Roasted Spareribs with Apple Sauce and Prunes

Mashed Potatoes, Brussel Sprouts, Red Cabbage, Carrots and Peas

"Pot Liquor" (the stock in which the ham and sausages have been cooked; see page 64)

Boiled "Lutfisk" with melted Butter, White or Mustard Sauce and Boiled Potatoes. Sometimes Peas are also served with "Lutfisk".

Christmas Rice Porridge with Cinnamon and Milk.

The good Christmas food is arranged on an attractively decorated large table (see illustration facing page 24). Brännvin and Christmas Beer are served. It is an old custom to have a large kettle of hot "Pot Liquor" standing on the stove into which everyone dips a few slices of bread. This "Dip in the Pot" is supposed to be a great delicacy. Sometimes different kinds of jam and cookies such as Christmas Crullers, Almond Tarts or the like are served as dessert.

Goose Dinner

St. Martin's Day is celebrated on November 11 in memory of a saint who died on that date. This celebration is maintained particularly in southern Sweden. How to set a goose dinner table, see illustration on page 49.

Black Soup and Goose Liver Sausage

Roast Goose and Red Cabbage, Apples and Prunes, Browned Potatoes

Fruit Salad.

English Index

Swedish Index

A CATALOG OF SELECTED
DOVER BOOKS
IN ALL FIELDS OF INTEREST

A CATALOG OF SELECTED DOVER BOOKS IN ALL FIELDS OF INTEREST

CONCERNING THE SPIRITUAL IN ART, Wassily Kandinsky. Pioneering work by father of abstract art. Thoughts on color theory, nature of art. Analysis of earlier masters. 12 illustrations. 80pp. of text. 5⅜ x 8½. 23411-8 Pa. $4.95

ANIMALS: 1,419 Copyright-Free Illustrations of Mammals, Birds, Fish, Insects, etc., Jim Harter (ed.). Clear wood engravings present, in extremely lifelike poses, over 1,000 species of animals. One of the most extensive pictorial sourcebooks of its kind. Captions. Index. 284pp. 9 x 12. 23766-4 Pa. $14.95

CELTIC ART: The Methods of Construction, George Bain. Simple geometric techniques for making Celtic interlacements, spirals, Kells-type initials, animals, humans, etc. Over 500 illustrations. 160pp. 9 x 12. (Available in U.S. only.) 22923-8 Pa. $9.95

AN ATLAS OF ANATOMY FOR ARTISTS, Fritz Schider. Most thorough reference work on art anatomy in the world. Hundreds of illustrations, including selections from works by Vesalius, Leonardo, Goya, Ingres, Michelangelo, others. 593 illustrations. 192pp. 7⅛ x 10¼. 20241-0 Pa. $9.95

CELTIC HAND STROKE-BY-STROKE (Irish Half-Uncial from "The Book of Kells"): An Arthur Baker Calligraphy Manual, Arthur Baker. Complete guide to creating each letter of the alphabet in distinctive Celtic manner. Covers hand position, strokes, pens, inks, paper, more. Illustrated. 48pp. 8¼ x 11. 24336-2 Pa. $3.95

EASY ORIGAMI, John Montroll. Charming collection of 32 projects (hat, cup, pelican, piano, swan, many more) specially designed for the novice origami hobbyist. Clearly illustrated easy-to-follow instructions insure that even beginning papercrafters will achieve successful results. 48pp. 8¼ x 11. 27298-2 Pa. $3.50

THE COMPLETE BOOK OF BIRDHOUSE CONSTRUCTION FOR WOODWORKERS, Scott D. Campbell. Detailed instructions, illustrations, tables. Also data on bird habitat and instinct patterns. Bibliography. 3 tables. 63 illustrations in 15 figures. 48pp. 5¼ x 8½. 24407-5 Pa. $2.50

BLOOMINGDALE'S ILLUSTRATED 1886 CATALOG: Fashions, Dry Goods and Housewares, Bloomingdale Brothers. Famed merchants' extremely rare catalog depicting about 1,700 products: clothing, housewares, firearms, dry goods, jewelry, more. Invaluable for dating, identifying vintage items. Also, copyright-free graphics for artists, designers. Co-published with Henry Ford Museum & Greenfield Village. 160pp. 8¼ x 11. 25780-0 Pa. $10.95

HISTORIC COSTUME IN PICTURES, Braun & Schneider. Over 1,450 costumed figures in clearly detailed engravings–from dawn of civilization to end of 19th century. Captions. Many folk costumes. 256pp. 8⅜ x 11¾. 23150-X Pa. $12.95

CATALOG OF DOVER BOOKS

STICKLEY CRAFTSMAN FURNITURE CATALOGS, Gustav Stickley and L. & J. G. Stickley. Beautiful, functional furniture in two authentic catalogs from 1910. 594 illustrations, including 277 photos, show settles, rockers, armchairs, reclining chairs, bookcases, desks, tables. 183pp. 6½ x 9¼. 23838-5 Pa. $11.95

AMERICAN LOCOMOTIVES IN HISTORIC PHOTOGRAPHS: 1858 to 1949, Ron Ziel (ed.). A rare collection of 126 meticulously detailed official photographs, called "builder portraits," of American locomotives that majestically chronicle the rise of steam locomotive power in America. Introduction. Detailed captions. xi+ 129pp. 9 x 12. 27393-8 Pa. $13.95

AMERICA'S LIGHTHOUSES: An Illustrated History, Francis Ross Holland, Jr. Delightfully written, profusely illustrated fact-filled survey of over 200 American lighthouses since 1716. History, anecdotes, technological advances, more. 240pp. 8 x 10¾. 25576-X Pa. $12.95

TOWARDS A NEW ARCHITECTURE, Le Corbusier. Pioneering manifesto by founder of "International School." Technical and aesthetic theories, views of industry, economics, relation of form to function, "mass-production split" and much more. Profusely illustrated. 320pp. 6⅛ x 9¼. (Available in U.S. only.) 25023-7 Pa. $10.95

HOW THE OTHER HALF LIVES, Jacob Riis. Famous journalistic record, exposing poverty and degradation of New York slums around 1900, by major social reformer. 100 striking and influential photographs. 233pp. 10 x 7⅞. 22012-5 Pa. $11.95

FRUIT KEY AND TWIG KEY TO TREES AND SHRUBS, William M. Harlow. One of the handiest and most widely used identification aids. Fruit key covers 120 deciduous and evergreen species; twig key 160 deciduous species. Easily used. Over 300 photographs. 126pp. 5⅜ x 8½. 20511-8 Pa. $3.95

COMMON BIRD SONGS, Dr. Donald J. Borror. Songs of 60 most common U.S. birds: robins, sparrows, cardinals, bluejays, finches, more—arranged in order of increasing complexity. Up to 9 variations of songs of each species. Cassette and manual 99911-4 $8.95

ORCHIDS AS HOUSE PLANTS, Rebecca Tyson Northen. Grow cattleyas and many other kinds of orchids—in a window, in a case, or under artificial light. 63 illustrations. 148pp. 5⅜ x 8½. 23261-1 Pa. $7.95

MONSTER MAZES, Dave Phillips. Masterful mazes at four levels of difficulty. Avoid deadly perils and evil creatures to find magical treasures. Solutions for all 32 exciting illustrated puzzles. 48pp. 8¼ x 11. 26005-4 Pa. $2.95

MOZART'S DON GIOVANNI (DOVER OPERA LIBRETTO SERIES), Wolfgang Amadeus Mozart. Introduced and translated by Ellen H. Bleiler. Standard Italian libretto, with complete English translation. Convenient and thoroughly portable—an ideal companion for reading along with a recording or the performance itself. Introduction. List of characters. Plot summary. 121pp. 5¼ x 8½. 24944-1 Pa. $3.95

TECHNICAL MANUAL AND DICTIONARY OF CLASSICAL BALLET, Gail Grant. Defines, explains, comments on steps, movements, poses and concepts. 15-page pictorial section. Basic book for student, viewer. 127pp. 5⅜ x 8½. 21843-0 Pa. $4.95

THE CLARINET AND CLARINET PLAYING, David Pino. Lively, comprehensive work features suggestions about technique, musicianship, and musical interpretation, as well as guidelines for teaching, making your own reeds, and preparing for public performance. Includes an intriguing look at clarinet history. "A godsend," *The Clarinet,* Journal of the International Clarinet Society. Appendixes. 7 illus. 320pp. 5⅜ x 8½. 40270-3 Pa. $9.95

HOLLYWOOD GLAMOR PORTRAITS, John Kobal (ed.). 145 photos from 1926-49. Harlow, Gable, Bogart, Bacall; 94 stars in all. Full background on photographers, technical aspects. 160pp. 8⅜ x 11¼. 23352-9 Pa. $12.95

THE ANNOTATED CASEY AT THE BAT: A Collection of Ballads about the Mighty Casey/Third, Revised Edition, Martin Gardner (ed.). Amusing sequels and parodies of one of America's best-loved poems: Casey's Revenge, Why Casey Whiffed, Casey's Sister at the Bat, others. 256pp. 5⅜ x 8½. 28598-7 Pa. $8.95

THE RAVEN AND OTHER FAVORITE POEMS, Edgar Allan Poe. Over 40 of the author's most memorable poems: "The Bells," "Ulalume," "Israfel," "To Helen," "The Conqueror Worm," "Eldorado," "Annabel Lee," many more. Alphabetic lists of titles and first lines. 64pp. 5$\frac{3}{16}$ x 8¼. 26685-0 Pa. $1.00

PERSONAL MEMOIRS OF U. S. GRANT, Ulysses Simpson Grant. Intelligent, deeply moving firsthand account of Civil War campaigns, considered by many the finest military memoirs ever written. Includes letters, historic photographs, maps and more. 528pp. 6⅛ x 9¼. 28587-1 Pa. $12.95

ANCIENT EGYPTIAN MATERIALS AND INDUSTRIES, A. Lucas and J. Harris. Fascinating, comprehensive, thoroughly documented text describes this ancient civilization's vast resources and the processes that incorporated them in daily life, including the use of animal products, building materials, cosmetics, perfumes and incense, fibers, glazed ware, glass and its manufacture, materials used in the mummification process, and much more. 544pp. 6⅛ x 9¼. (Available in U.S. only.) 40446-3 Pa. $16.95

RUSSIAN STORIES/PYCCKNE PACCKA3bl: A Dual-Language Book, edited by Gleb Struve. Twelve tales by such masters as Chekhov, Tolstoy, Dostoevsky, Pushkin, others. Excellent word-for-word English translations on facing pages, plus teaching and study aids, Russian/English vocabulary, biographical/critical introductions, more. 416pp. 5⅜ x 8½. 26244-8 Pa. $9.95

PHILADELPHIA THEN AND NOW: 60 Sites Photographed in the Past and Present, Kenneth Finkel and Susan Oyama. Rare photographs of City Hall, Logan Square, Independence Hall, Betsy Ross House, other landmarks juxtaposed with contemporary views. Captures changing face of historic city. Introduction. Captions. 128pp. 8¼ x 11. 25790-8 Pa. $9.95

AIA ARCHITECTURAL GUIDE TO NASSAU AND SUFFOLK COUNTIES, LONG ISLAND, The American Institute of Architects, Long Island Chapter, and the Society for the Preservation of Long Island Antiquities. Comprehensive, well-researched and generously illustrated volume brings to life over three centuries of Long Island's great architectural heritage. More than 240 photographs with authoritative, extensively detailed captions. 176pp. 8¼ x 11. 26946-9 Pa. $14.95

NORTH AMERICAN INDIAN LIFE: Customs and Traditions of 23 Tribes, Elsie Clews Parsons (ed.). 27 fictionalized essays by noted anthropologists examine religion, customs, government, additional facets of life among the Winnebago, Crow, Zuni, Eskimo, other tribes. 480pp. 6⅛ x 9¼. 27377-6 Pa. $10.95

FRANK LLOYD WRIGHT'S DANA HOUSE, Donald Hoffmann. Pictorial essay of residential masterpiece with over 160 interior and exterior photos, plans, elevations, sketches and studies. 128pp. 9¼ x 10¾. 29120-0 Pa. $14.95

THE MALE AND FEMALE FIGURE IN MOTION: 60 Classic Photographic Sequences, Eadweard Muybridge. 60 true-action photographs of men and women walking, running, climbing, bending, turning, etc., reproduced from rare 19th-century masterpiece. vi + 121pp. 9 x 12. 24745-7 Pa. $12.95

1001 QUESTIONS ANSWERED ABOUT THE SEASHORE, N. J. Berrill and Jacquelyn Berrill. Queries answered about dolphins, sea snails, sponges, starfish, fishes, shore birds, many others. Covers appearance, breeding, growth, feeding, much more. 305pp. 5¼ x 8¼. 23366-9 Pa. $9.95

ATTRACTING BIRDS TO YOUR YARD, William J. Weber. Easy-to-follow guide offers advice on how to attract the greatest diversity of birds: birdhouses, feeders, water and waterers, much more. 96pp. 5³⁄₁₆ x 8¼. 28927-3 Pa. $2.50

MEDICINAL AND OTHER USES OF NORTH AMERICAN PLANTS: A Historical Survey with Special Reference to the Eastern Indian Tribes, Charlotte Erichsen-Brown. Chronological historical citations document 500 years of usage of plants, trees, shrubs native to eastern Canada, northeastern U.S. Also complete identifying information. 343 illustrations. 544pp. 6½ x 9¼. 25951-X Pa. $12.95

STORYBOOK MAZES, Dave Phillips. 23 stories and mazes on two-page spreads: Wizard of Oz, Treasure Island, Robin Hood, etc. Solutions. 64pp. 8¼ x 11. 23628-5 Pa. $2.95

AMERICAN NEGRO SONGS: 230 Folk Songs and Spirituals, Religious and Secular, John W. Work. This authoritative study traces the African influences of songs sung and played by black Americans at work, in church, and as entertainment. The author discusses the lyric significance of such songs as "Swing Low, Sweet Chariot," "John Henry," and others and offers the words and music for 230 songs. Bibliography. Index of Song Titles. 272pp. 6½ x 9¼. 40271-1 Pa. $9.95

MOVIE-STAR PORTRAITS OF THE FORTIES, John Kobal (ed.). 163 glamor, studio photos of 106 stars of the 1940s: Rita Hayworth, Ava Gardner, Marlon Brando, Clark Gable, many more. 176pp. 8⅜ x 11¼. 23546-7 Pa. $14.95

BENCHLEY LOST AND FOUND, Robert Benchley. Finest humor from early 30s, about pet peeves, child psychologists, post office and others. Mostly unavailable elsewhere. 73 illustrations by Peter Arno and others. 183pp. 5⅜ x 8½. 22410-4 Pa. $6.95

YEKL and THE IMPORTED BRIDEGROOM AND OTHER STORIES OF YIDDISH NEW YORK, Abraham Cahan. Film Hester Street based on *Yekl* (1896). Novel, other stories among first about Jewish immigrants on N.Y.'s East Side. 240pp. 5⅜ x 8½. 22427-9 Pa. $7.95

SELECTED POEMS, Walt Whitman. Generous sampling from *Leaves of Grass*. Twenty-four poems include "I Hear America Singing," "Song of the Open Road," "I Sing the Body Electric," "When Lilacs Last in the Dooryard Bloom'd," "O Captain! My Captain!"–all reprinted from an authoritative edition. Lists of titles and first lines. 128pp. 5³⁄₁₆ x 8¼. 26878-0 Pa. $1.00

THE BEST TALES OF HOFFMANN, E. T. A. Hoffmann. 10 of Hoffmann's most important stories: "Nutcracker and the King of Mice," "The Golden Flowerpot," etc. 458pp. 5⅜ x 8½. 21793-0 Pa. $9.95

FROM FETISH TO GOD IN ANCIENT EGYPT, E. A. Wallis Budge. Rich detailed survey of Egyptian conception of "God" and gods, magic, cult of animals, Osiris, more. Also, superb English translations of hymns and legends. 240 illustrations. 545pp. 5⅜ x 8½. 25803-3 Pa. $13.95

FRENCH STORIES/CONTES FRANÇAIS: A Dual-Language Book, Wallace Fowlie. Ten stories by French masters, Voltaire to Camus: "Micromegas" by Voltaire; "The Atheist's Mass" by Balzac; "Minuet" by de Maupassant; "The Guest" by Camus, six more. Excellent English translations on facing pages. Also French-English vocabulary list, exercises, more. 352pp. 5⅜ x 8½. 26443-2 Pa. $9.95

CHICAGO AT THE TURN OF THE CENTURY IN PHOTOGRAPHS: 122 Historic Views from the Collections of the Chicago Historical Society, Larry A. Viskochil. Rare large-format prints offer detailed views of City Hall, State Street, the Loop, Hull House, Union Station, many other landmarks, circa 1904-1913. Introduction. Captions. Maps. 144pp. 9⅜ x 12¼. 24656-6 Pa. $12.95

OLD BROOKLYN IN EARLY PHOTOGRAPHS, 1865-1929, William Lee Younger. Luna Park, Gravesend race track, construction of Grand Army Plaza, moving of Hotel Brighton, etc. 157 previously unpublished photographs. 165pp. 8⅞ x 11¾. 23587-4 Pa. $13.95

THE MYTHS OF THE NORTH AMERICAN INDIANS, Lewis Spence. Rich anthology of the myths and legends of the Algonquins, Iroquois, Pawnees and Sioux, prefaced by an extensive historical and ethnological commentary. 36 illustrations. 480pp. 5⅜ x 8½. 25967-6 Pa. $10.95

AN ENCYCLOPEDIA OF BATTLES: Accounts of Over 1,560 Battles from 1479 B.C. to the Present, David Eggenberger. Essential details of every major battle in recorded history from the first battle of Megiddo in 1479 B.C. to Grenada in 1984. List of Battle Maps. New Appendix covering the years 1967-1984. Index. 99 illustrations. 544pp. 6½ x 9¼. 24913-1 Pa. $16.95

SAILING ALONE AROUND THE WORLD, Captain Joshua Slocum. First man to sail around the world, alone, in small boat. One of great feats of seamanship told in delightful manner. 67 illustrations. 294pp. 5⅜ x 8½. 20326-3 Pa. $6.95

ANARCHISM AND OTHER ESSAYS, Emma Goldman. Powerful, penetrating, prophetic essays on direct action, role of minorities, prison reform, puritan hypocrisy, violence, etc. 271pp. 5⅜ x 8½. 22484-8 Pa. $8.95

MYTHS OF THE HINDUS AND BUDDHISTS, Ananda K. Coomaraswamy and Sister Nivedita. Great stories of the epics; deeds of Krishna, Shiva, taken from puranas, Vedas, folk tales; etc. 32 illustrations. 400pp. 5⅜ x 8½. 21759-0 Pa. $12.95

THE TRAUMA OF BIRTH, Otto Rank. Rank's controversial thesis that anxiety neurosis is caused by profound psychological trauma which occurs at birth. 256pp. 5⅜ x 8½. 27974-X Pa. $7.95

A THEOLOGICO-POLITICAL TREATISE, Benedict Spinoza. Also contains unfinished Political Treatise. Great classic on religious liberty, theory of government on common consent. R. Elwes translation. Total of 421pp. 5⅜ x 8½. 20249-6 Pa. $10.95

MY BONDAGE AND MY FREEDOM, Frederick Douglass. Born a slave, Douglass became outspoken force in antislavery movement. The best of Douglass' autobiographies. Graphic description of slave life. 464pp. 5⅜ x 8½. 22457-0 Pa. $8.95

FOLLOWING THE EQUATOR: A Journey Around the World, Mark Twain. Fascinating humorous account of 1897 voyage to Hawaii, Australia, India, New Zealand, etc. Ironic, bemused reports on peoples, customs, climate, flora and fauna, politics, much more. 197 illustrations. 720pp. 5⅜ x 8½. 26113-1 Pa. $15.95

THE PEOPLE CALLED SHAKERS, Edward D. Andrews. Definitive study of Shakers: origins, beliefs, practices, dances, social organization, furniture and crafts, etc. 33 illustrations. 351pp. 5⅜ x 8½. 21081-2 Pa. $12.95

THE MYTHS OF GREECE AND ROME, H. A. Guerber. A classic of mythology, generously illustrated, long prized for its simple, graphic, accurate retelling of the principal myths of Greece and Rome, and for its commentary on their origins and significance. With 64 illustrations by Michelangelo, Raphael, Titian, Rubens, Canova, Bernini and others. 480pp. 5⅜ x 8½. 27584-1 Pa. $10.95

PSYCHOLOGY OF MUSIC, Carl E. Seashore. Classic work discusses music as a medium from psychological viewpoint. Clear treatment of physical acoustics, auditory apparatus, sound perception, development of musical skills, nature of musical feeling, host of other topics. 88 figures. 408pp. 5⅜ x 8½. 21851-1 Pa. $11.95

THE PHILOSOPHY OF HISTORY, Georg W. Hegel. Great classic of Western thought develops concept that history is not chance but rational process, the evolution of freedom. 457pp. 5⅜ x 8½. 20112-0 Pa. $9.95

THE BOOK OF TEA, Kakuzo Okakura. Minor classic of the Orient: entertaining, charming explanation, interpretation of traditional Japanese culture in terms of tea ceremony. 94pp. 5⅜ x 8½. 20070-1 Pa. $3.95

LIFE IN ANCIENT EGYPT, Adolf Erman. Fullest, most thorough, detailed older account with much not in more recent books, domestic life, religion, magic, medicine, commerce, much more. Many illustrations reproduce tomb paintings, carvings, hieroglyphs, etc. 597pp. 5⅜ x 8½. 22632-8 Pa. $12.95

SUNDIALS, Their Theory and Construction, Albert Waugh. Far and away the best, most thorough coverage of ideas, mathematics concerned, types, construction, adjusting anywhere. Simple, nontechnical treatment allows even children to build several of these dials. Over 100 illustrations. 230pp. 5⅜ x 8½. 22947-5 Pa. $8.95

THEORETICAL HYDRODYNAMICS, L. M. Milne-Thomson. Classic exposition of the mathematical theory of fluid motion, applicable to both hydrodynamics and aerodynamics. Over 600 exercises. 768pp. 6⅛ x 9¼. 68970-0 Pa. $20.95

SONGS OF EXPERIENCE: Facsimile Reproduction with 26 Plates in Full Color, William Blake. 26 full-color plates from a rare 1826 edition. Includes "The Tyger," "London," "Holy Thursday," and other poems. Printed text of poems. 48pp. 5¼ x 7. 24636-1 Pa. $4.95

OLD-TIME VIGNETTES IN FULL COLOR, Carol Belanger Grafton (ed.). Over 390 charming, often sentimental illustrations, selected from archives of Victorian graphics—pretty women posing, children playing, food, flowers, kittens and puppies, smiling cherubs, birds and butterflies, much more. All copyright-free. 48pp. 9¼ x 12¼. 27269-9 Pa. $7.95

PERSPECTIVE FOR ARTISTS, Rex Vicat Cole. Depth, perspective of sky and sea, shadows, much more, not usually covered. 391 diagrams, 81 reproductions of drawings and paintings. 279pp. 5⅜ x 8½. 22487-2 Pa. $9.95

DRAWING THE LIVING FIGURE, Joseph Sheppard. Innovative approach to artistic anatomy focuses on specifics of surface anatomy, rather than muscles and bones. Over 170 drawings of live models in front, back and side views, and in widely varying poses. Accompanying diagrams. 177 illustrations. Introduction. Index. 144pp. 8⅜ x11¼. 26723-7 Pa. $9.95

GOTHIC AND OLD ENGLISH ALPHABETS: 100 Complete Fonts, Dan X. Solo. Add power, elegance to posters, signs, other graphics with 100 stunning copyright-free alphabets: Blackstone, Dolbey, Germania, 97 more–including many lower-case, numerals, punctuation marks. 104pp. 8⅛ x 11. 24695-7 Pa. $9.95

HOW TO DO BEADWORK, Mary White. Fundamental book on craft from simple projects to five-bead chains and woven works. 106 illustrations. 142pp. 5⅜ x 8. 20697-1 Pa. $5.95

THE BOOK OF WOOD CARVING, Charles Marshall Sayers. Finest book for beginners discusses fundamentals and offers 34 designs. "Absolutely first rate . . . well thought out and well executed."–E. J. Tangerman. 118pp. 7¾ x 10⅝. 23654-4 Pa. $7.95

ILLUSTRATED CATALOG OF CIVIL WAR MILITARY GOODS: Union Army Weapons, Insignia, Uniform Accessories, and Other Equipment, Schuyler, Hartley, and Graham. Rare, profusely illustrated 1846 catalog includes Union Army uniform and dress regulations, arms and ammunition, coats, insignia, flags, swords, rifles, etc. 226 illustrations. 160pp. 9 x 12. 24939-5 Pa. $12.95

WOMEN'S FASHIONS OF THE EARLY 1900s: An Unabridged Republication of "New York Fashions, 1909," National Cloak & Suit Co. Rare catalog of mail-order fashions documents women's and children's clothing styles shortly after the turn of the century. Captions offer full descriptions, prices. Invaluable resource for fashion, costume historians. Approximately 725 illustrations. 128pp. 8⅜ x 11¼. 27276-1 Pa. $12.95

THE 1912 AND 1915 GUSTAV STICKLEY FURNITURE CATALOGS, Gustav Stickley. With over 200 detailed illustrations and descriptions, these two catalogs are essential reading and reference materials and identification guides for Stickley furniture. Captions cite materials, dimensions and prices. 112pp. 6½ x 9¼. 26676-1 Pa. $9.95

EARLY AMERICAN LOCOMOTIVES, John H. White, Jr. Finest locomotive engravings from early 19th century: historical (1804–74), main-line (after 1870), special, foreign, etc. 147 plates. 142pp. 11⅜ x 8¼. 22772-3 Pa. $12.95

THE TALL SHIPS OF TODAY IN PHOTOGRAPHS, Frank O. Braynard. Lavishly illustrated tribute to nearly 100 majestic contemporary sailing vessels: Amerigo Vespucci, Clearwater, Constitution, Eagle, Mayflower, Sea Cloud, Victory, many more. Authoritative captions provide statistics, background on each ship. 190 black-and-white photographs and illustrations. Introduction. 128pp. 8⅞ x 11¾. 27163-3 Pa. $14.95

CATALOG OF DOVER BOOKS

LITTLE BOOK OF EARLY AMERICAN CRAFTS AND TRADES, Peter Stockham (ed.). 1807 children's book explains crafts and trades: baker, hatter, cooper, potter, and many others. 23 copperplate illustrations. 140pp. 4 5/8 x 6.
23336-7 Pa. $4.95

VICTORIAN FASHIONS AND COSTUMES FROM HARPER'S BAZAR, 1867–1898, Stella Blum (ed.). Day costumes, evening wear, sports clothes, shoes, hats, other accessories in over 1,000 detailed engravings. 320pp. 9 3/8 x 12 1/4.
22990-4 Pa. $16.95

GUSTAV STICKLEY, THE CRAFTSMAN, Mary Ann Smith. Superb study surveys broad scope of Stickley's achievement, especially in architecture. Design philosophy, rise and fall of the Craftsman empire, descriptions and floor plans for many Craftsman houses, more. 86 black-and-white halftones. 31 line illustrations. Introduction 208pp. 6 1/2 x 9 1/4. 27210-9 Pa. $9.95

THE LONG ISLAND RAIL ROAD IN EARLY PHOTOGRAPHS, Ron Ziel. Over 220 rare photos, informative text document origin (1844) and development of rail service on Long Island. Vintage views of early trains, locomotives, stations, passengers, crews, much more. Captions. 8 7/8 x 11 3/4. 26301-0 Pa. $14.95

VOYAGE OF THE LIBERDADE, Joshua Slocum. Great 19th-century mariner's thrilling, first-hand account of the wreck of his ship off South America, the 35-foot boat he built from the wreckage, and its remarkable voyage home. 128pp. 5 3/8 x 8 1/2.
40022-0 Pa. $5.95

TEN BOOKS ON ARCHITECTURE, Vitruvius. The most important book ever written on architecture. Early Roman aesthetics, technology, classical orders, site selection, all other aspects. Morgan translation. 331pp. 5 3/8 x 8 1/2. 20645-9 Pa. $9.95

THE HUMAN FIGURE IN MOTION, Eadweard Muybridge. More than 4,500 stopped-action photos, in action series, showing undraped men, women, children jumping, lying down, throwing, sitting, wrestling, carrying, etc. 390pp. 7 7/8 x 10 5/8.
20204-6 Clothbd. $29.95

TREES OF THE EASTERN AND CENTRAL UNITED STATES AND CANADA, William M. Harlow. Best one-volume guide to 140 trees. Full descriptions, woodlore, range, etc. Over 600 illustrations. Handy size. 288pp. 4 1/2 x 6 3/8.
20395-6 Pa. $6.95

SONGS OF WESTERN BIRDS, Dr. Donald J. Borror. Complete song and call repertoire of 60 western species, including flycatchers, juncoes, cactus wrens, many more–includes fully illustrated booklet. Cassette and manual 99913-0 $8.95

GROWING AND USING HERBS AND SPICES, Milo Miloradovich. Versatile handbook provides all the information needed for cultivation and use of all the herbs and spices available in North America. 4 illustrations. Index. Glossary. 236pp. 5 3/8 x 8 1/2.
25058-X Pa. $7.95

BIG BOOK OF MAZES AND LABYRINTHS, Walter Shepherd. 50 mazes and labyrinths in all–classical, solid, ripple, and more–in one great volume. Perfect inexpensive puzzler for clever youngsters. Full solutions. 112pp. 8 1/8 x 11.
22951-3 Pa. $5.95

PIANO TUNING, J. Cree Fischer. Clearest, best book for beginner, amateur. Simple repairs, raising dropped notes, tuning by easy method of flattened fifths. No previous skills needed. 4 illustrations. 201pp. 5⅜ x 8½. 23267-0 Pa. $6.95

HINTS TO SINGERS, Lillian Nordica. Selecting the right teacher, developing confidence, overcoming stage fright, and many other important skills receive thoughtful discussion in this indispensible guide, written by a world-famous diva of four decades' experience. 96pp. 5⅜ x 8½. 40094-8 Pa. $4.95

THE COMPLETE NONSENSE OF EDWARD LEAR, Edward Lear. All nonsense limericks, zany alphabets, Owl and Pussycat, songs, nonsense botany, etc., illustrated by Lear. Total of 320pp. 5⅜ x 8½. (Available in U.S. only.) 20167-8 Pa. $7.95

VICTORIAN PARLOUR POETRY: An Annotated Anthology, Michael R. Turner. 117 gems by Longfellow, Tennyson, Browning, many lesser-known poets. "The Village Blacksmith," "Curfew Must Not Ring Tonight," "Only a Baby Small," dozens more, often difficult to find elsewhere. Index of poets, titles, first lines. xxiii + 325pp. 5⅝ x 8¼. 27044-0 Pa. $12.95

DUBLINERS, James Joyce. Fifteen stories offer vivid, tightly focused observations of the lives of Dublin's poorer classes. At least one, "The Dead," is considered a masterpiece. Reprinted complete and unabridged from standard edition. 160pp. 5³⁄₁₆ x 8¼. 26870-5 Pa. $1.50

GREAT WEIRD TALES: 14 Stories by Lovecraft, Blackwood, Machen and Others, S. T. Joshi (ed.). 14 spellbinding tales, including "The Sin Eater," by Fiona McLeod, "The Eye Above the Mantel," by Frank Belknap Long, as well as renowned works by R. H. Barlow, Lord Dunsany, Arthur Machen, W. C. Morrow and eight other masters of the genre. 256pp. 5⅜ x 8½. (Available in U.S. only.) 40436-6 Pa. $8.95

THE BOOK OF THE SACRED MAGIC OF ABRAMELIN THE MAGE, translated by S. MacGregor Mathers. Medieval manuscript of ceremonial magic. Basic document in Aleister Crowley, Golden Dawn groups. 268pp. 5⅜ x 8½. 23211-5 Pa. $9.95

NEW RUSSIAN-ENGLISH AND ENGLISH-RUSSIAN DICTIONARY, M. A. O'Brien. This is a remarkably handy Russian dictionary, containing a surprising amount of information, including over 70,000 entries. 366pp. 4½ x 6⅛. 20208-9 Pa. $10.95

HISTORIC HOMES OF THE AMERICAN PRESIDENTS, Second, Revised Edition, Irvin Haas. A traveler's guide to American Presidential homes, most open to the public, depicting and describing homes occupied by every American President from George Washington to George Bush. With visiting hours, admission charges, travel routes. 175 photographs. Index. 160pp. 8¼ x 11. 26751-2 Pa. $13.95

NEW YORK IN THE FORTIES, Andreas Feininger. 162 brilliant photographs by the well-known photographer, formerly with *Life* magazine. Commuters, shoppers, Times Square at night, much else from city at its peak. Captions by John von Hartz. 181pp. 9¼ x 10¾. 23585-8 Pa. $13.95

INDIAN SIGN LANGUAGE, William Tomkins. Over 525 signs developed by Sioux and other tribes. Written instructions and diagrams. Also 290 pictographs. 111pp. 6⅛ x 9¼. 22029-X Pa. $3.95

ANATOMY: A Complete Guide for Artists, Joseph Sheppard. A master of figure drawing shows artists how to render human anatomy convincingly. Over 460 illustrations. 224pp. 8⅜ x 11¼. 27279-6 Pa. $11.95

MEDIEVAL CALLIGRAPHY: Its History and Technique, Marc Drogin. Spirited history, comprehensive instruction manual covers 13 styles (ca. 4th century through 15th). Excellent photographs; directions for duplicating medieval techniques with modern tools. 224pp. 8⅜ x 11¼. 26142-5 Pa. $12.95

DRIED FLOWERS: How to Prepare Them, Sarah Whitlock and Martha Rankin. Complete instructions on how to use silica gel, meal and borax, perlite aggregate, sand and borax, glycerine and water to create attractive permanent flower arrangements. 12 illustrations. 32pp. 5⅜ x 8½. 21802-3 Pa. $1.00

EASY-TO-MAKE BIRD FEEDERS FOR WOODWORKERS, Scott D. Campbell. Detailed, simple-to-use guide for designing, constructing, caring for and using feeders. Text, illustrations for 12 classic and contemporary designs. 96pp. 5⅜ x 8½. 25847-5 Pa. $3.95

SCOTTISH WONDER TALES FROM MYTH AND LEGEND, Donald A. Mackenzie. 16 lively tales tell of giants rumbling down mountainsides, of a magic wand that turns stone pillars into warriors, of gods and goddesses, evil hags, powerful forces and more. 240pp. 5⅜ x 8½. 29677-6 Pa. $6.95

THE HISTORY OF UNDERCLOTHES, C. Willett Cunnington and Phyllis Cunnington. Fascinating, well-documented survey covering six centuries of English undergarments, enhanced with over 100 illustrations: 12th-century laced-up bodice, footed long drawers (1795), 19th-century bustles, 19th-century corsets for men, Victorian "bust improvers," much more. 272pp. 5⅝ x 8¼. 27124-2 Pa. $9.95

ARTS AND CRAFTS FURNITURE: The Complete Brooks Catalog of 1912, Brooks Manufacturing Co. Photos and detailed descriptions of more than 150 now very collectible furniture designs from the Arts and Crafts movement depict davenports, settees, buffets, desks, tables, chairs, bedsteads, dressers and more, all built of solid, quarter-sawed oak. Invaluable for students and enthusiasts of antiques, Americana and the decorative arts. 80pp. 6½ x 9¼. 27471-3 Pa. $8.95

WILBUR AND ORVILLE: A Biography of the Wright Brothers, Fred Howard. Definitive, crisply written study tells the full story of the brothers' lives and work. A vividly written biography, unparalleled in scope and color, that also captures the spirit of an extraordinary era. 560pp. 6⅛ x 9¼. 40297-5 Pa. $17.95

THE ARTS OF THE SAILOR: Knotting, Splicing and Ropework, Hervey Garrett Smith. Indispensable shipboard reference covers tools, basic knots and useful hitches; handsewing and canvas work, more. Over 100 illustrations. Delightful reading for sea lovers. 256pp. 5⅜ x 8½. 26440-8 Pa. $8.95

FRANK LLOYD WRIGHT'S FALLINGWATER: The House and Its History, Second, Revised Edition, Donald Hoffmann. A total revision–both in text and illustrations–of the standard document on Fallingwater, the boldest, most personal architectural statement of Wright's mature years, updated with valuable new material from the recently opened Frank Lloyd Wright Archives. "Fascinating"–*The New York Times*. 116 illustrations. 128pp. 9¼ x 10¾. 27430-6 Pa. $12.95

PHOTOGRAPHIC SKETCHBOOK OF THE CIVIL WAR, Alexander Gardner. 100 photos taken on field during the Civil War. Famous shots of Manassas Harper's Ferry, Lincoln, Richmond, slave pens, etc. 244pp. 10⅝ x 8¼. 22731-6 Pa. $10.95

FIVE ACRES AND INDEPENDENCE, Maurice G. Kains. Great back-to-the-land classic explains basics of self-sufficient farming. The one book to get. 95 illustrations. 397pp. 5⅜ x 8½. 20974-1 Pa. $7.95

SONGS OF EASTERN BIRDS, Dr. Donald J. Borror. Songs and calls of 60 species most common to eastern U.S.: warblers, woodpeckers, flycatchers, thrushes, larks, many more in high-quality recording. Cassette and manual 99912-2 $9.95

A MODERN HERBAL, Margaret Grieve. Much the fullest, most exact, most useful compilation of herbal material. Gigantic alphabetical encyclopedia, from aconite to zedoary, gives botanical information, medical properties, folklore, economic uses, much else. Indispensable to serious reader. 161 illustrations. 888pp. 6½ x 9¼. 2-vol. set. (Available in U.S. only.) Vol. I: 22798-7 Pa. $10.95
Vol. II: 22799-5 Pa. $10.95

HIDDEN TREASURE MAZE BOOK, Dave Phillips. Solve 34 challenging mazes accompanied by heroic tales of adventure. Evil dragons, people-eating plants, blood-thirsty giants, many more dangerous adversaries lurk at every twist and turn. 34 mazes, stories, solutions. 48pp. 8¼ x 11. 24566-7 Pa. $2.95

LETTERS OF W. A. MOZART, Wolfgang A. Mozart. Remarkable letters show bawdy wit, humor, imagination, musical insights, contemporary musical world; includes some letters from Leopold Mozart. 276pp. 5⅜ x 8½. 22859-2 Pa. $9.95

BASIC PRINCIPLES OF CLASSICAL BALLET, Agrippina Vaganova. Great Russian theoretician, teacher explains methods for teaching classical ballet. 118 illustrations. 175pp. 5⅜ x 8½. 22036-2 Pa. $6.95

THE JUMPING FROG, Mark Twain. Revenge edition. The original story of The Celebrated Jumping Frog of Calaveras County, a hapless French translation, and Twain's hilarious "retranslation" from the French. 12 illustrations. 66pp. 5⅜ x 8½. 22686-7 Pa. $4.95

BEST REMEMBERED POEMS, Martin Gardner (ed.). The 126 poems in this superb collection of 19th- and 20th-century British and American verse range from Shelley's "To a Skylark" to the impassioned "Renascence" of Edna St. Vincent Millay and to Edward Lear's whimsical "The Owl and the Pussycat." 224pp. 5⅜ x 8½. 27165-X Pa. $5.95

COMPLETE SONNETS, William Shakespeare. Over 150 exquisite poems deal with love, friendship, the tyranny of time, beauty's evanescence, death and other themes in language of remarkable power, precision and beauty. Glossary of archaic terms. 80pp. 5³⁄₁₆ x 8¼. 26686-9 Pa. $1.00

THE BATTLES THAT CHANGED HISTORY, Fletcher Pratt. Eminent historian profiles 16 crucial conflicts, ancient to modern, that changed the course of civilization. 352pp. 5⅜ x 8½. 41129-X Pa. $9.95

THE WIT AND HUMOR OF OSCAR WILDE, Alvin Redman (ed.). More than 1,000 ripostes, paradoxes, wisecracks: Work is the curse of the drinking classes; I can resist everything except temptation; etc. 258pp. 5⅜ x 8½. 20602-5 Pa. $6.95

SHAKESPEARE LEXICON AND QUOTATION DICTIONARY, Alexander Schmidt. Full definitions, locations, shades of meaning in every word in plays and poems. More than 50,000 exact quotations. 1,485pp. 6½ x 9¼. 2-vol. set.
Vol. 1: 22726-X Pa. $17.95
Vol. 2: 22727-8 Pa. $17.95

SELECTED POEMS, Emily Dickinson. Over 100 best-known, best-loved poems by one of America's foremost poets, reprinted from authoritative early editions. No comparable edition at this price. Index of first lines. 64pp. 5³⁄₁₆ x 8¼.
26466-1 Pa. $1.00

THE INSIDIOUS DR. FU-MANCHU, Sax Rohmer. The first of the popular mystery series introduces a pair of English detectives to their archnemesis, the diabolical Dr. Fu-Manchu. Flavorful atmosphere, fast-paced action, and colorful characters enliven this classic of the genre. 208pp. 5³⁄₁₆ x 8¼. 29898-1 Pa. $2.00

THE MALLEUS MALEFICARUM OF KRAMER AND SPRENGER, translated by Montague Summers. Full text of most important witchhunter's "bible," used by both Catholics and Protestants. 278pp. 6⅝ x 10. 22802-9 Pa. $12.95

SPANISH STORIES/CUENTOS ESPAÑOLES: A Dual-Language Book, Angel Flores (ed.). Unique format offers 13 great stories in Spanish by Cervantes, Borges, others. Faithful English translations on facing pages. 352pp. 5⅜ x 8½.
25399-6 Pa. $8.95

GARDEN CITY, LONG ISLAND, IN EARLY PHOTOGRAPHS, 1869–1919, Mildred H. Smith. Handsome treasury of 118 vintage pictures, accompanied by carefully researched captions, document the Garden City Hotel fire (1899), the Vanderbilt Cup Race (1908), the first airmail flight departing from the Nassau Boulevard Aerodrome (1911), and much more. 96pp. 8⅞ x 11¾. 40669-5 Pa. $12.95

OLD QUEENS, N.Y., IN EARLY PHOTOGRAPHS, Vincent F. Seyfried and William Asadorian. Over 160 rare photographs of Maspeth, Jamaica, Jackson Heights, and other areas. Vintage views of DeWitt Clinton mansion, 1939 World's Fair and more. Captions. 192pp. 8⅞ x 11. 26358-4 Pa. $14.95

CAPTURED BY THE INDIANS: 15 Firsthand Accounts, 1750-1870, Frederick Drimmer. Astounding true historical accounts of grisly torture, bloody conflicts, relentless pursuits, miraculous escapes and more, by people who lived to tell the tale. 384pp. 5⅜ x 8½. 24901-8 Pa. $9.95

THE WORLD'S GREAT SPEECHES (Fourth Enlarged Edition), Lewis Copeland, Lawrence W. Lamm, and Stephen J. McKenna. Nearly 300 speeches provide public speakers with a wealth of updated quotes and inspiration—from Pericles' funeral oration and William Jennings Bryan's "Cross of Gold Speech" to Malcolm X's powerful words on the Black Revolution and Earl of Spenser's tribute to his sister, Diana, Princess of Wales. 944pp. 5⅜ x 8⅜. 40903-1 Pa. $15.95

THE BOOK OF THE SWORD, Sir Richard F. Burton. Great Victorian scholar/adventurer's eloquent, erudite history of the "queen of weapons"—from prehistory to early Roman Empire. Evolution and development of early swords, variations (sabre, broadsword, cutlass, scimitar, etc.), much more. 336pp. 6⅛ x 9¼.
25434-8 Pa. $9.95

AUTOBIOGRAPHY: The Story of My Experiments with Truth, Mohandas K. Gandhi. Boyhood, legal studies, purification, the growth of the Satyagraha (nonviolent protest) movement. Critical, inspiring work of the man responsible for the freedom of India. 480pp. 5⅜ x 8½. (Available in U.S. only.) 24593-4 Pa. $9.95

CELTIC MYTHS AND LEGENDS, T. W. Rolleston. Masterful retelling of Irish and Welsh stories and tales. Cuchulain, King Arthur, Deirdre, the Grail, many more. First paperback edition. 58 full-page illustrations. 512pp. 5⅜ x 8½. 26507-2 Pa. $9.95

THE PRINCIPLES OF PSYCHOLOGY, William James. Famous long course complete, unabridged. Stream of thought, time perception, memory, experimental methods; great work decades ahead of its time. 94 figures. 1,391pp. 5⅜ x 8½. 2-vol. set.
Vol. I: 20381-6 Pa. $14.95
Vol. II: 20382-4 Pa. $14.95

THE WORLD AS WILL AND REPRESENTATION, Arthur Schopenhauer. Definitive English translation of Schopenhauer's life work, correcting more than 1,000 errors, omissions in earlier translations. Translated by E. F. J. Payne. Total of 1,269pp. 5⅜ x 8½. 2-vol. set.
Vol. 1: 21761-2 Pa. $12.95
Vol. 2: 21762-0 Pa. $12.95

MAGIC AND MYSTERY IN TIBET, Madame Alexandra David-Neel. Experiences among lamas, magicians, sages, sorcerers, Bonpa wizards. A true psychic discovery. 32 illustrations. 321pp. 5⅜ x 8½. (Available in U.S. only.) 22682-4 Pa. $9.95

THE EGYPTIAN BOOK OF THE DEAD, E. A. Wallis Budge. Complete reproduction of Ani's papyrus, finest ever found. Full hieroglyphic text, interlinear transliteration, word-for-word translation, smooth translation. 533pp. 6½ x 9¼.
21866-X Pa. $12.95

MATHEMATICS FOR THE NONMATHEMATICIAN, Morris Kline. Detailed, college-level treatment of mathematics in cultural and historical context, with numerous exercises. Recommended Reading Lists. Tables. Numerous figures. 641pp. 5⅜ x 8½.
24823-2 Pa. $11.95

PROBABILISTIC METHODS IN THE THEORY OF STRUCTURES, Isaac Elishakoff. Well-written introduction covers the elements of the theory of probability from two or more random variables, the reliability of such multivariable structures, the theory of random function, Monte Carlo methods of treating problems incapable of exact solution, and more. Examples. 502pp. 5³/₈ x 8¹/₂. 40691-1 Pa. $16.95

THE RIME OF THE ANCIENT MARINER, Gustave Doré, S. T. Coleridge. Doré's finest work; 34 plates capture moods, subtleties of poem. Flawless full-size reproductions printed on facing pages with authoritative text of poem. "Beautiful. Simply beautiful."–*Publisher's Weekly.* 77pp. 9¼ x 12. 22305-1 Pa. $7.95

NORTH AMERICAN INDIAN DESIGNS FOR ARTISTS AND CRAFTSPEOPLE, Eva Wilson. Over 360 authentic copyright-free designs adapted from Navajo blankets, Hopi pottery, Sioux buffalo hides, more. Geometrics, symbolic figures, plant and animal motifs, etc. 128pp. 8⅜ x 11. (Not for sale in the United Kingdom.) 25341-4 Pa. $9.95

SCULPTURE: Principles and Practice, Louis Slobodkin. Step-by-step approach to clay, plaster, metals, stone; classical and modern. 253 drawings, photos. 255pp. 8⅛ x 11.
22960-2 Pa. $11.95

CATALOG OF DOVER BOOKS

THE INFLUENCE OF SEA POWER UPON HISTORY, 1660–1783, A. T. Mahan. Influential classic of naval history and tactics still used as text in war colleges. First paperback edition. 4 maps. 24 battle plans. 640pp. 5⅜ x 8½. 25509-3 Pa. $14.95

THE STORY OF THE TITANIC AS TOLD BY ITS SURVIVORS, Jack Winocour (ed.). What it was really like. Panic, despair, shocking inefficiency, and a little heroism. More thrilling than any fictional account. 26 illustrations. 320pp. 5⅜ x 8½. 20610-6 Pa. $8.95

FAIRY AND FOLK TALES OF THE IRISH PEASANTRY, William Butler Yeats (ed.). Treasury of 64 tales from the twilight world of Celtic myth and legend: "The Soul Cages," "The Kildare Pooka," "King O'Toole and his Goose," many more. Introduction and Notes by W. B. Yeats. 352pp. 5⅜ x 8½. 26941-8 Pa. $8.95

BUDDHIST MAHAYANA TEXTS, E. B. Cowell and others (eds.). Superb, accurate translations of basic documents in Mahayana Buddhism, highly important in history of religions. The Buddha-karita of Asvaghosha, Larger Sukhavativyuha, more. 448pp. 5⅜ x 8½. 25552-2 Pa. $12.95

ONE TWO THREE . . . INFINITY: Facts and Speculations of Science, George Gamow. Great physicist's fascinating, readable overview of contemporary science: number theory, relativity, fourth dimension, entropy, genes, atomic structure, much more. 128 illustrations. Index. 352pp. 5⅜ x 8½. 25664-2 Pa. $9.95

EXPERIMENTATION AND MEASUREMENT, W. J. Youden. Introductory manual explains laws of measurement in simple terms and offers tips for achieving accuracy and minimizing errors. Mathematics of measurement, use of instruments, experimenting with machines. 1994 edition. Foreword. Preface. Introduction. Epilogue. Selected Readings. Glossary. Index. Tables and figures. 128pp. 5³/₈ x 8¹/₂. 40451-X Pa. $6.95

DALÍ ON MODERN ART: The Cuckolds of Antiquated Modern Art, Salvador Dalí. Influential painter skewers modern art and its practitioners. Outrageous evaluations of Picasso, Cézanne, Turner, more. 15 renderings of paintings discussed. 44 calligraphic decorations by Dalí. 96pp. 5⅜ x 8½. (Available in U.S. only.) 29220-7 Pa. $5.95

ANTIQUE PLAYING CARDS: A Pictorial History, Henry René D'Allemagne. Over 900 elaborate, decorative images from rare playing cards (14th–20th centuries): Bacchus, death, dancing dogs, hunting scenes, royal coats of arms, players cheating, much more. 96pp. 9¼ x 12¼. 29265-7 Pa. $12.95

MAKING FURNITURE MASTERPIECES: 30 Projects with Measured Drawings, Franklin H. Gottshall. Step-by-step instructions, illustrations for constructing handsome, useful pieces, among them a Sheraton desk, Chippendale chair, Spanish desk, Queen Anne table and a William and Mary dressing mirror. 224pp. 8⅛ x 11¼. 29338-6 Pa. $13.95

THE FOSSIL BOOK: A Record of Prehistoric Life, Patricia V. Rich et al. Profusely illustrated definitive guide covers everything from single-celled organisms and dinosaurs to birds and mammals and the interplay between climate and man. Over 1,500 illustrations. 760pp. 7½ x 10⅛. 29371-8 Pa. $29.95

Prices subject to change without notice.